About a mile and a half east of Sand Springs was the junction where passenger trolleys of the Sand Springs Railway usually met. Car 71 is heading toward Sand Springs and will traverse a clockwise loop ending up back at this junction. Car 70, right, has just completed the loop and is bound for Tulsa. Track at right was abandoned at end of passenger service in 1955.

William D. Middleton

When OKLAHOMA Took THE Trolley

Interurbans Special 71

Allison Chandler and Stephen D. Maguire

with Mac Sebree

When Oklahoma Took the Trolley

Library of Congress Catalog Number: 79-92539

ISBN: 0-916374-35-1

Design and layout by Bill Bradley

Interurbans
P.O. Box 6444 Glendale, California 91205

Mac Sebree, *President*
Jim Walker, *Vice President*

Foreword

I HAVE ALWAYS felt that Oklahoma packed more traction diversity per square mile than any other midwestern or southwestern state. Naturally, those who rode the Illinois Terminal and the vast Chicago Surface Lines system, sped to Milwaukee on the Electroliner, or saw the Indianapolis Traction Terminal in its prime, might disagree. But I am prejudiced: I lived in the Sooner State for better than a decade and enjoyed the experience thoroughly. The state has an exuberance and a vitality that was captured pretty well in the Rogers and Hammerstein super-hit Musical *Oklahoma!* The exclamation point was not put in by accident.

Furthermore, I was around when the Oklahoma Railway was still running its rail rapid transit line to Norman (no hicktown country trolley line, this) and the Sand Springs line was still dispatching its yellow trolleys out of Tulsa every 20 minutes as if it intended to do so forever. I walked every foot of the Tulsa-Sapulpa Union when it still had a trolley wire over it, and spent hours examining the track cracks in the brick streets of Muskogee. All this in addition to running a wire service news bureau and chasing news stories all over the state.

When Allison Chandler and Stephen D. Maguire offered the fruits of their textual and photographic researches on the Sooner State as a part of a contemplated multi-state traction anthology, Interurbans felt ill-prepared to tackle such a large subject until Publisher Sebree got into the act and began to envision a sentimental journey through so many Oklahoma yesterdays. Would the authors, we asked, consider letting us publish a single book only on Oklahoma, possibly augmented by other sources from Sebree's own background, but based solidly on the many years of work already performed by Chandler and Maguire? The answer was affirmative, and so away we went and here we are with a photo and fact narrative on the halcyon times when Oklahomans would sooner take the trolley. (Pardon the pun; at least we didn't put that on the cover.)

The authors are indebted to many individuals and institutions for assistance, and editor Sebree likewise drew upon some old sources. Photographers are individually credited in the book, but special mention should be made of the contribution of William D. Middleton who shared his file on the Sand Springs Railway, much of which went into a *Trains*

Double-truck Birney car of the Sand Springs Railway crosses the trestle at Sand Springs Park en route to Tulsa on August 22, 1954. Sadly, this photo could not be repeated the following summer because all passenger service was abandoned in January 1955.
William D. Middleton

Magazine article, and to Fred W. Schneider III who not only printed Middleton's photos but contributed many of his own, and from such collections as Bill Janssen and Robert Mehlenbeck.

Then there was some additional research done by Sebree to Oklahoma in the Fall of 1978. With a slight amount of trading on old friendships he was able to rummage through the newspaper morgues of the *Tulsa World and Tribune,* the *Daily Oklahoman and Times,* and the *Oklahoma Journal* in Oklahoma City. Individual thanks goes to Alex Adwan and Phil Dessauer of the *Tulsa World,* J. Bob Lucas of the *Tulsa Tribune* (an old Muskogee hand), Deacon New of the *Daily Oklahoman,* Harry Culver of United Press International, and John Clabes and Bill Tharp of the *Journal.*

Another very helpful source was Charles E. Winters of Kansas City, Mo., who has access to the John B. Fink Collection of the University of Oklahoma. Mr. Fink traveled around the state back in the 1930s and aimed his camera at everything that looked interesting. That included a lot of trolley cars.

No doubt we have inadvertently left someone out; for that we apologize in advance. But here is a list of helpful individuals and organizations:

Joe H. Barber, Bartlesville
A.E. Bauman, Enid
Wilma N. Berry, Bartlesville Public Library
Carl B. Blaubach, Walnut Creek, Calif.
Charlene Browning, Clinton Public Library
Mrs. John C. Doan, Okmulgee Public Library
Beryl D. Ford, Tulsa
Preston George, Edmond
Mrs. Zoe Gigoux, Lawton Carnegie Public Library
Griggs Studio, Bartlesville
Floyd M. Gurley, Belen, N.M.
Elsie P. Hannan, Ardmore Public Library
Willa Grace Hardy, Cushing Public Library
Dan Harris, Enid
Mrs. Velma Hayne, Enid
Earl R. Holloway, Ardmore
Jess Jordan, Western Trails Museum, Clinton
Ernest C. Lambert, Okmulgee
Gordon Lloyd, Pittsburgh, Pa.
Prof. George W. Hilton, Los Angeles, Calif.

L.D. Moore, Chesapeake, Virginia
William A. (Mac) McGalliard, Ardmore
Warren Miller, Railway Negative Exchange, Moraga, Calif.
Forrest D. Monahan, Jr., Wichita Falls, Texas
Jerry Moore, Tulsa
Irwin Munn, Chickasha
Museum of the Cherokee Strip, Lawton
Johnnie Myers, Fort Worth, Texas
Oklahoma Historical Society, Oklahoma City
Wayne Phillips, Webbers Falls Public Library
Dee Ann Ray, Western Plains Library System, Clinton
Felix E. Reifschneider, Fairton, N.J.
Steve Scalzo, Chicago, Ill.
Charles Smallwood, San Francisco, Calif.
Oakla Mount Spears, Okmulgee
R.B. Strong, Jr., Clinton
Theodore P. Taetsch, Half Moon Bay, Calif.
Mrs. Phil J. Wells, Cushing, Okla.
Rod Varney, Texas Division, Electric Railroaders Assn., San Antonio, Texas
Avery Von Blon, Waco, Texas
Jim Walker, Glendale, Calif.
Jackie White, Clinton

Of the individuals named above, we would like to add a special word or two about Oakla Mount Spears, who, with her husband, both retired ranchers, volunteered on short notice to do some deep digging into the history of the very obscure Okmulgee system and proceeded to come up with a great deal of data and a couple of rare photos. And then, when the editor was having some trouble with Muskogee, insisted on doing the same work in the neighboring city.

And, as always, Rod Varney of the Texas ERA unselfishly made available his division file on Oklahoma, which was extensive.

So we give you Oklahoma: a state whose economy has in large measure been dependent on oil, which fueled the streetcar's competitor, but which at the same time nurtured for so long such an interesting and productive variety of streetcar and interurban systems.

—MAC SEBREE

Contents

Maps

Introduction

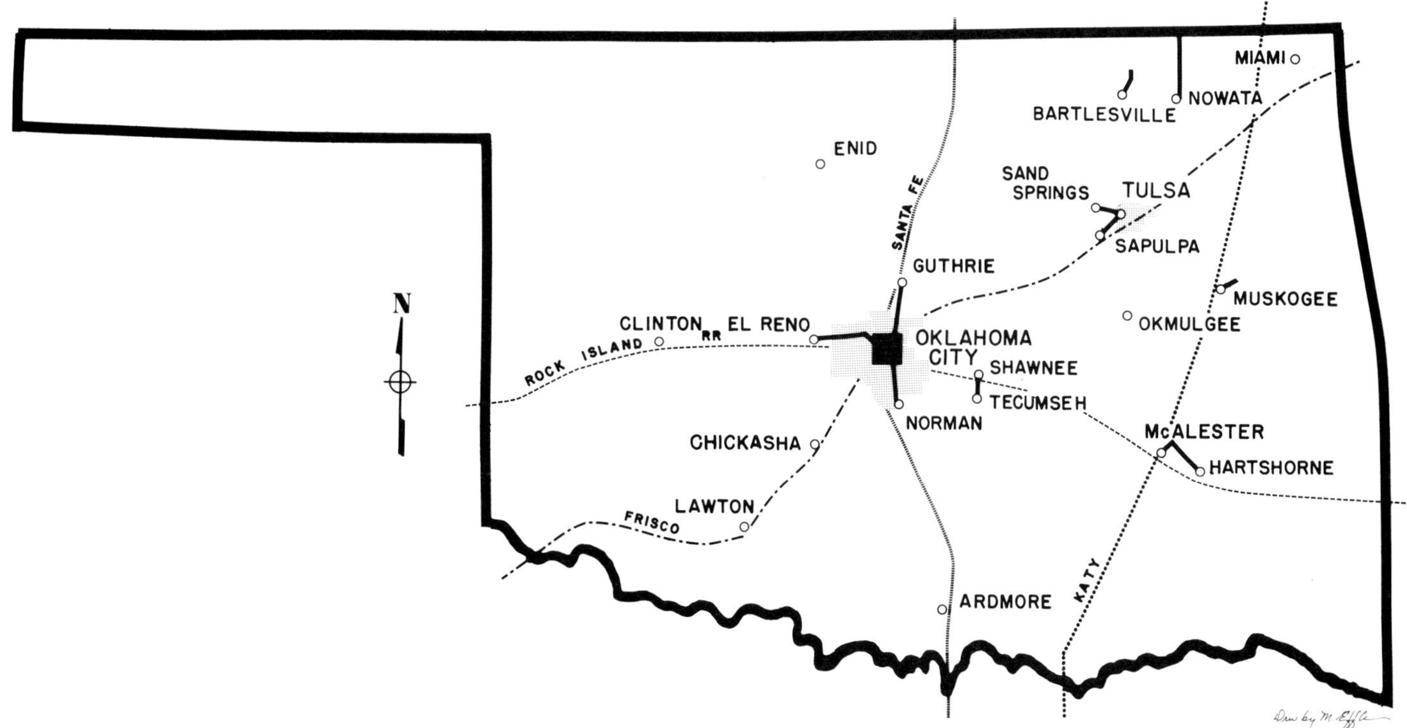

OKLAHOMA has always had a good transportation network. Mainline railroads and a thick network of branches link the state with the rest of the nation, and the state's large wheat crop and other agricultural commodities move from crossroads elevator to market efficiently by the Santa Fe, Rock Island, Frisco, Katy and other railroads. In former years, a considerable amount of railroad passenger service was offered but, alas, even Amtrak's *Lone Star,* the final train serving Soonerland, along the Santa Fe north and south through Oklahoma City, was discontinued in October 1978.

Likewise, a network of paved highways was built up over the years. If not always maintained in tiptop shape, the "slab" at least reached into every nook and cranny of the state. Starting in the 1950s, the free highway network was supplemented by a system of toll roads, the first of which was the Turner Turnpike between Oklahoma City and Tulsa. This anticipated the limited-access Interstate highway system by a good 10 years, and was made necessary due to the tendency in Oklahoma for even the major highways to be only two-lane, often running at right angles to the direct, diagonal routes between major centers.

A unique institution in the Sooner State was a very early system of fast express routes, pioneered by the electric inter-urbans but soon overtaken by trucks of the state's two major morning daily newspapers. Mistletoe Express, operated by the Oklahoma Publishing Co., and Magic Empire Express, by the Tulsa World, were outgrowths of the newspapers' own delivery routes and gave the state a small package service not matched elsewhere until the rise of United Parcel.

This book tells the story of another transportation network, now all but forgotten. In better days, Oklahoma was well endowed with electric railways. At one time the streetcar and the interurban were a major factor in the state's economy. There was a time when political battles were fought over routes and franchises, when paving disputes between hard-pressed trolley operators and irate city councils made weekly headlines, when proposals for a penny increase in carfare set off citizens' revolts. The electric cars touched our lives intimately.

While the trolley has stayed alive (and is even in for a revival) in some states, and in the rest of the world generally, it has left the home of the oil rig, the Big Red football team and the corn that is as high as an elephant's eye. Let us celebrate, in these few pages, a colorful era in the Sooner State's past, when Oklahoma Took the Trolley.

Rocking through the weeds, Guthrie-bound interurban 224 gingerly enters the siding at Blucher to let a southbound car pass. It was an overcast September 12, 1938, when this photo was taken.   *William C. Janssen*

Oklahoma Railway Company

1. RAILS TO THE BIG CITY

O KLAHOMA'S largest, most important and most modern electric railway served the capital city and three important outlying cities for some four decades with an efficiently operated city and interurban transit service. Although rail service was finally abandoned in 1947 it might have carried on much longer if circumstances had been slightly more favorable.

Considering that Oklahoma City's population in the 1920s was only some 125,000 people, the Oklahoma Railway Co. offered extensive service on its city lines and the interurbans to Norman, Guthrie and El Reno. It spent lavishly to upgrade its operations late in the decade, bought new cars and expanded heavily into freight operations, even building a 10-mile, $1 million freight belt bypass line around the western edge of the city.

The result was that Oklahoma City enjoyed a public transportation system unusually elaborate for a city of its size. The investment proved to be a mixed blessing for the company itself. And, eventually, the city lost its fine transit facilities even as its population doubled and tripled in the aftermath of World War II.

In 1902, Oklahoma City was not yet the capital of Oklahoma and its population was only some 14,000. On January 28 of that year the Metropolitan Railway Co. was chartered; its organizers were W.W. Storm, John W. Shartel, S.T. Alton, E.H. Cooke and John Threadgill.

The original plan called for a four-mile double-tracked loop around the downtown district on Main Street and Grand Ave., but by February 7, 1903, cars were operated on a more elaborate system including a line from Choctaw and Broadway north to 13th and Broadway; a line from Main and Broadway west to Western; a line from Reno and Harvey north to Fourth, west to Walker and north to 13th, and a line to Stiles Park from Fourth and Broadway via Harrison Ave.

On June 15, 1904, the Oklahoma City Railway Co. was incorporated to succeed the Metropolitan; the original five trolleys were augmented by additional rolling stock. Then, on September 21, 1907, the Oklahoma Railway Co., parent firm to the OCR, began using its own name on the cars. Although the firm had ties to St. Louis financiers, it was not connected with a power company.

ORC's first president was Anton H. Classen with Shartel serving as first vice president. Both men gave their names to major Oklahoma City traffic arteries which were also streetcar routes. By 1910 the Classen Blvd. line was built to the north edge of the city at Belle Isle. Here a large power plant was built.

Traction power had been obtained in the early years from the same plant which furnished light and power to city homes and businesses. But as the city grew it became necessary to cut off certain residential sections after dark to handle downtown lighting and the streetcars (this would be known today as "rolling brownouts"). Finally the superintendent of the power company decided that lights were more important than trolleys, so when the electrical load grew too heavy he cut off the streetcar circuit, leaving cars stranded.

So Oklahoma Railway built its own power plant at Belle Isle, and from 1908 until 1928 produced its own power. An amusement park was also constructed at Belle Isle as a traffic stimulator.

In 1909 the ORC acquired 29 pieces of rolling stock from manufacturers and built two work locomotives in the company shop; trackage now totaled 32 miles. The first interurban, a line to Guthrie (31 miles), was planned and the tracks had already reached Britton, eight miles north. Rolling stock included 46 passenger cars.

On April 1, 1910, ORC acquired the lines of the Oklahoma City & Suburban Railway Co., which operated 25 miles of trackage. This brought company lines to all parts of town.

Another independent enterprise taken over was the El Reno Interurban Railway Co., which had been organized in 1909, operated a small El Reno city system and was building west on what is now 39th Street from Classen Blvd. to the suburb of Yukon. The Oklahoma Railway purchased the ERIR on August 1, 1911, and completed the line all the way

Early day predecessor to ORC was the Oklahoma City Railway Co., whose single-trucker No. 9 was captured by the photographer back around 1909.
Oklahoma Journal

to El Reno (29 miles), opening through-service on December 3, 1911.

The beginnings of the highly important interurban to Norman dated from 1910, when the Capitol Hill line was extended to Moore, nine miles south of the city. Meanwhile, gross passenger earnings of the railway rose from $440,846 in 1909 to $623,887 in 1910, easing off slightly to $620,092 in 1911. In 1912, the Britton line was extended through open country to Edmond, 15 miles north and site of a state teachers' college. In that year the company's lines totaled 103 miles, on which operated 95 passenger cars, two electric locomotives and 22 freight and dump cars.

It was in November of 1913 that Oklahoma Railway cars finally reached Norman, home of the University of Oklahoma. This was the shortest of ORC's three interurban lines (18 miles in length), but by far the busiest and remained so to the end.

Finally, on July 20, 1916 (rather late in the era of interurban construction in the U.S.), the interurban system was completed with the beginning of revenue service into Guthrie, the old territorial capital which had lost the title to Oklahoma City upon statehood, and located 31 miles north of the latter.

Now, the system totaled 138.2 miles and was in its era of greatest expansion. More than 50 new cars were purchased in the period 1913-1918, a freight business was being built up, amusement centers at Belle Isle, Briarwood, the Fair Grounds and Wheeler Park were drawing streetcar crowds, and excess electric energy was being sold to consumers.

Business on all three interurban lines was essentially suburban in character, but the Norman line excelled in terminal-to-terminal traffic, especially for students bound to and from the state university. Typically, passenger schedules were on an hourly basis, although in the 1930s headways on the Guthrie and El Reno lines were changed to every 90 minutes, while the Norman line service was improved to half-hourly.

Oklahoma City's population, which had been 65,000 in 1910, hit 92,000 in 1920. The company, with its resources drained by the extensive construction program during the previous decade, encountered financial difficulties even prior to a 1921 recession. Despite the new cars, service was slow, routings were awkward and traffic congestion was harming streetcar performance.

From 1911, a large passenger and freight terminal at Grand Ave. and Hudson, downtown, had been the Oklahoma Railway's nerve center. The original layout included four through loading tracks and four stub tracks. Both city and interurban cars used the terminal. Because of growing congestion, the layout was revised in 1924 to include four through tracks for city cars and two through tracks for interurbans. Many cities had interurban terminals, but Oklahoma City was one of the few to route all local cars through the station as well.

This was but one of many Oklahoma Railway operations studied carefully in 1925 by the engineering firm of Stone & Webster. That firm made several recommendations, including new cars, restricted parking rules for autos, and through routing for many of the city lines which would remove them from the congested terminal.

By this time, ORC was in receivership with George A. Henshaw in charge of operations. The receiver followed many of Stone & Webster's recommendations, and discontinued use of the terminal for local cars. The company also persuaded the state legislature to permit street railways to

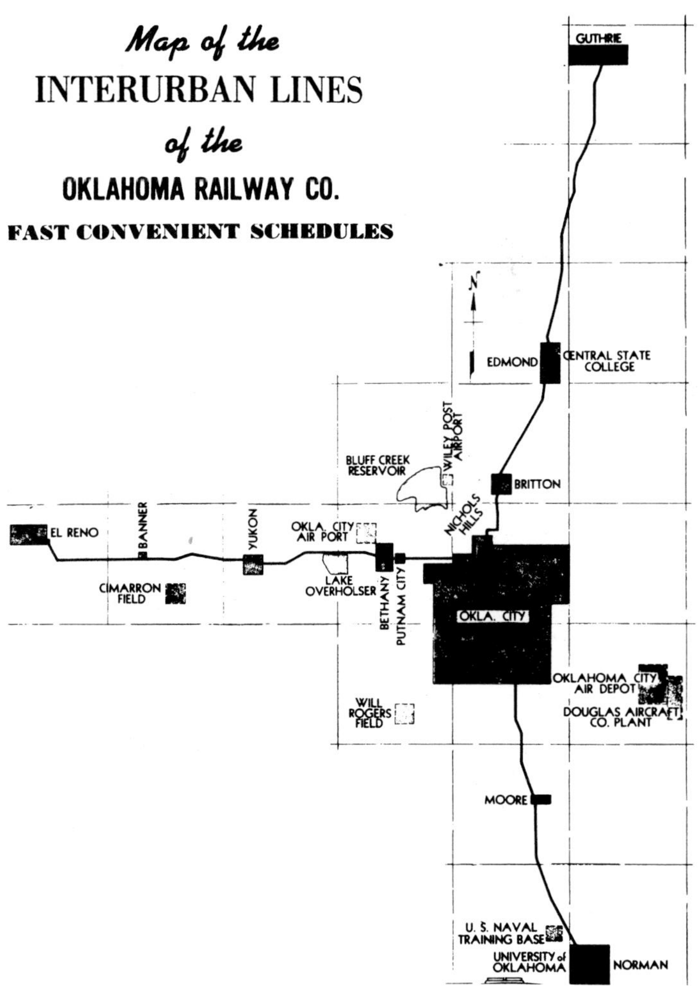

Map shows ORC interurban lines extending north, west and south.   *Oklahoma Railway Co.*

operate buses; ORC put its first bus line in operation in 1925.

The affairs of the Oklahoma Railway took a dramatic turn for the better in 1927. Major increases in ridership began to be felt in 1926, and in the following year the company was sold to a local group headed by Hubert R. Hudson. His associates included William Mee, banker; Dr. G.A. Nichols, real estate promoter (most noted for development of his exclusive Nichols Hills subdivision north of the city); T.C. Thatcher, miller; A.E. Monroney, furniture store owner and father of the later U.S. Senator A.S. Mike Monroney; and A.O. Campbell, contractor.

The new management was dynamic. It promptly sold the Belle Isle power plant to the Oklahoma Gas & Electric Co., bought the Oklahoma Belt Railroad Co., and leased the Oklahoma City Junction Railway to create a network of freight belt lines in the southern part of the city, serving the stockyards and packing-house district.

Within two years, ORC spent $2 million to buy new streetcars and buses, extend lines, build a new carhouse and shops, and electrify the two railroad belt lines it had bought.

Since the only really modern passenger cars on the property were 20 single-truck Birney safety cars purchased in 1923, the new management ordered 10 new double-truck, one-man cars for delivery in 1929 along with six new buses. In 1930, the company followed up with 20 more new cars, 10 single-end and 10 double-end.

The downtown streetcar terminal was remodeled once again, and the previous management's decision to route

On the college run in 1937, this 1930-built city car still looked factory-fresh as it negotiated Grand Ave. half a block from the interurban terminal.
Texas ERA Collection

local streetcars away from it was revoked. Once again, local passengers could change cars and buses in the Grand Ave. terminal.

The old car shops at Second and Olie were torn down, and replaced by a new facility at Noble and Exchange, on the Packingtown car line. The company spent $250,000 on the new facilities, located on the site of an old amusement park. Besides a modern carhouse, the complex included a paint shop, carpenter shop and bus garage.

Perhaps the boldest move the new owners made was to try to capture a goodly share of all local freight switching and terminal business. In addition to buying and leasing the two belt lines, ORC built an entirely new freight line, a west side belt along Grand Blvd., actually an unimproved boulevard more or less encircling the entire city but existing mostly on maps.

Together with a shorter bypass route around the old Belle Isle park and lake, the new line tied together all three of the company's interurban lines and removed freight trains from city trackage. Residents along Classen Blvd., one of the city's more prestigious thoroughfares, had been complaining about the noise and congestion of freight trains for years.

The city was so glad to get rid of the freight trains that it agreed to give up to the ORC a strip of right-of-way on Grand Blvd., which originally had been planned as a residential parkway but which still was far beyond the end of the built-up residential area.

The new line was put into operation in December of 1928, passing directly by the new shop complex on Exchange Ave., linking up with the Norman interurban line in the Capitol Hill district. It also connected with the Santa Fe, Frisco and Rock Island mainline railroads. The company planned to offer passenger service on the new belt line, but the area never built up enough to make this feasible.

To handle the new freight traffic, ORC built four more electric locomotives to add to the three already in service. Carload freight solicitation began in earnest, and through-traffic agreements were negotiated with major steam railroads. One such arrangement, with the Fort Smith & Western Railroad, provided a valuable interchange for mainline freight at Guthrie; when the latter railroad was abandoned in 1939, ORC's freight revenues suffered a major decline.

The new freight activity enabled the Oklahoma Railway to face the onset of the Great Depression with vigor. During this time the company served such important industries as the Armour and Swift packing plants, Capitol Steel & Iron Co., Oklahoma Gas & Electric Co., American Tank Co., Farmers City Public Market, Black, Sivalls & Bryson, Inc., and the Colbert Feed Pens.

Interstate Shipments To Every Point

CITY DELIVERY
To Convenient Team Tracks and Docks

Above is an actual photograph of one of the electric locomotives now in regular service.

TO THE SHIPPING PUBLIC

FROM SEABOARD TERRITORY: The Oklahoma Railway has an excellent merchandise arrangement from all seaboard territory in connection with rail and ocean routes. Shipments routed via Seaboard Norfolk Lines or Central Savannah Lines, care of Oklahoma Railway are assured the most reasonable freight rates and the most dependable time.

We maintain double daily service between all points on Guthrie and El Reno division making direct early morning and late evening connections at El Reno, Oklahoma, with the CRI&P Railway and at Guthrie, Oklahoma with the AT&SF and FS&W Railways, which affords prompt early morning or overnight delivery of all carloads to our patrons at Oklahoma City, and delivery to connections at Oklahoma City of shipments in switch service.

Express shipments handled every hour on passenger trains; it's faster than mail.

The Oklahoma Railway Company in connection with the KCS and FS&W Railways operates through package car daily from Kansas City to Oklahoma City, which gives our patrons second morning delivery of all merchandise via this route, also furnishes prompt fast service for shipments from Chicago, St. Louis and points East when routed via Kansas City, KCS, FS&W, Oklahoma Railway delivery.

POOL CAR SHIPPERS: Because of its Regular service, conveniently timed, the Oklahoma Railway can best finish the distribution of the pool car shipments made to Oklahoma City and distributed to the following points: Guthrie, Edmond, Britton, Moore, Norman, Bethany, Yukon, Banner and El Reno.

The Oklahoma Railway Company serves the greater industries and industrial districts of Oklahoma City.

FOR FURTHER INFORMATION: Ask any agent, or address—

Phone 3-7485
NEIL NORSWORTHY
Traffic Manager, Oklahoma Railway
Terminal Building, Oklahoma City

GEO. F. KLEINHOFFER
General Agent, Oklahoma Railway
307 Railway Ex. Bldg., Kansas City, Mo.
Phone Victor 2620

LOUIS FEIKERT
General Agent, Oklahoma Railway
409 Pierce Bldg., St. Louis, Mo.
Phone Main 2474

CLOSE CONNECTIONS AT EL RENO, GUTHRIE AND OKLAHOMA CITY WITH ALL RAILROADS

GENERAL INFORMATION

RATES: Following is a table of rates between Oklahoma City and principal points:

	One way	Round trip		One way	Round trip
Norman	$ .55	$1.00	Yukon	$ .50	$ .90
Edmond	.45	.85	Banner	.65	1.20
Guthrie	.95	1.75	El Reno	.90	1.65)

CHARTERED CARS AND BUSES: Given special attention. Party rates and service obtainable any time by chartering a car. These cars and buses start from and return to any point on city or Interurban lines, and time is arranged to suit your convenience. Our finest cars and buses are used for this service.

BAGGAGE: Baggage to the extent of 150 pounds will be checked free on all full fare, one-way, or round trip tickets, provided such fare equals twenty-five cents. If fare is less than twenty-five cents, baggage will be checked upon payment of difference between such fare and twenty-five cents. Baggage will be carried on all regular scheduled Interurban cars. Excess baggage will be carried at regular excess rates filed with the Corporation Commission of Oklahoma, and baggage may be checked to any depot or residence in Oklahoma City for a small additional charge. For particulars ask the agent.

Through tickets sold and baggage checked to all points on the Ft. S. & W. R. R.

The person who travels frequently in Oklahoma Railway territory has learned how much better and cheaper are the interurbans and buses than automobile transportation. Commutation books make big savings possible.

Oklahoma Railway Co.

Oklahoma Railway devoted a whole page in its 1930 passenger timetable extolling the virtues of its electric freight service.
Texas ERA Collection

Changing trolleys was end-of-line ritual. Here it is done on December 6, 1940, at the end of the North Robinson line in Oklahoma City.
John B. Fink Collection from Charles Winters

And, in addition to the Santa Fe, Frisco and Rock Island interchanges, the ORC made connections with the Oklahoma City-Ada-Atoka Railway and the Missouri-Kansas-Texas at Oklahoma City, and the Rock Island at Yukon, where two major flour mills were served.

So confident of the future was Oklahoma Railway that, on May 30, 1930, Hudson announced a major streetcar expansion plan. The company, he said, planned to build trackage on 23rd Street for a major crosstown route, and new trunk lines on South Western, North May, North Eastern from 23rd (then out in the country), North Penn from 12th, South Agnew from 25th and on South Robinson from Capitol Hill. He also announced an extension of the North Robinson line from 28th to 33rd streets.

But the Depression came on even more swiftly, and the company quickly and quietly dropped all mention of expansion, except for construction of the North Robinson extension which was finished late in the year.

From 1931 to 1933 company revenues plunged sharply, reaching in the latter year the lowest point since 1915. At the same time, the company was shifting emphasis steadily to the motor bus, and by January 1, 1931, the company was operating 54 of them. Business started to improve in 1934,

"Walkathons" were all the rage in the mid-1930s, something like marathon dancing, perhaps. Such an event was advertised on the front dash of Belle Isle car 131 heading out Classen Blvd. in the summer of 1934.
Robert V. Mehlenbeck

but took another nosedive during the recession of 1938, a period which followed a siege of drought and agricultural losses—the state's dark "dust bowl" days.

Something had to give—and once again it was the finances of the Oklahoma Railway Co. In July 1939, the company filed for reorganization under the bankruptcy act; on September 27 of that year Hudson and Robert K. Johnston were named trustees. Hudson died in March 1940, and Johnston served as sole trustee until 1943.

For the first time, the company undertook a major trimming of its rail network. On December 8, 1940, the Shartel, South Shields, North Robinson, and Broadway-17th lines were all abandoned, and the remaining lines were through-routed away from the interurban terminal. In May of 1941 the Lincoln Park line also was abandoned. Many new bus lines were started and the fleet enlarged to more than 150 by 1942.

The Grand Ave. interurban terminal was once again reserved exclusively for the Norman, Guthrie and El Reno cars. But they continued to run, and the terminal continued to be a busy place. Passengers, baggage, express and some freight were dispatched at all hours of the day and night amid the sounds of squealing flanges, traction gears, the thump of air compressors and the hiss of trolley wheels.

One unusual use of the Oklahoma Railway interurban network was recounted by Sam D. Hales, longtime Oklahoma manager and business representative of the United Press, whose bureau was located in the Black Hotel near the terminal. Most Oklahoma daily newspapers served by the UP were on telegraph lines or teleprinter circuits, but the *El Reno Daily Tribune,* the *Guthrie Leader* and the *Norman Transcript* had a more economical access to the UP's news reports: the interurban.

Every day except Sunday, a UP copyboy would gather up a sheaf of dispatches at two- or three-hour intervals, take the envelopes to the terminal and hand them up to the motormen of departing interurban cars. The cars were met at the other end of the line by staff members from the respective newspapers.

This operation ended when the interurbans did, but for several years ORC's red-and-cream interurbans were an integral part of the UP's worldwide news distribution network.

Japanese dive bombers propelled America into World War II on December 7, 1941. At this time Oklahoma Railway city trolleys—painted green and cream—served five routes: Belle Isle (Classen Blvd.) through-routed with State Capitol-Culberton; Fair Grounds, through-routed with Exchange-Stockyards, and the Linwood line, which looped downtown. This line had been shortened from 19th and Woodland to 12th and Drexel in 1940.

Because the three interurban lines were still operating,

Norman-bound,, car 219 threads the traffic on South Walker at Noble in May 1934.   *Robert V. Mehlenbeck*

along with the major Classen and State Capitol local lines, Oklahoma Railway was well able to cope with the major traffic increases of World War II. The Norman line, in particular, was overwhelmed, doubling to more than 40 runs daily with its half-hourly schedules sometimes operated in four or more sections.

This in turn placed impossible demands on ORC's dwindling electric car fleet, which was down to just 11 interurbans and about 40 city cars. The company turned to the used equipment market, and was able to come up with a number of serviceable cars cast off by abandoned systems in other parts of the country.

The dramatic increase in ORC fortunes is illustrated by contrasting the 39 schedules dispatched daily in 1941 with the 192 cars dispatched daily in 1944. The big increase on the Norman line was due not only to the university but to a pair of Naval bases established in the college town.

The Navy, in fact, came to ORC's rescue on the equipment market; in 1943 the USN acquired five interurbans from the Schenectady, N.Y., Railway and three more from the Dayton & Xenia in Ohio, and leased them to Oklahoma Railway. Other "boomer" cars operating on ORC rails included four from the Indiana Service Corporation, Fort Wayne, which had been added back in 1933, and seven cars from Rockford, Ill., in 1937.

Helping out on the city lines were 10, 1929-built cars acquired in 1936 from the Flint, Mich., Street Railway.

Altogether, by 1944, 28 cars including two rescued from roadside diner duty and four cars rebuilt from freight cars, were in interurban passenger service, struggling to carry record crowds.

On June 17, 1944, a tragic accident marred Oklahoma Railway's record of wartime traffic achievement. It was a rear-end collision of two passenger trains on the overtaxed Norman line, and resulted in the deaths of three passengers and one employe, and injury to 35.

Although part of the single-track Norman line was protected by block signals, a portion in the middle, which included the stop at Berry, 6.5 miles south of the Oklahoma City terminal station, was not.

More than 150 passengers boarded the four sections of train 258 due to leave Norman at 8:10 P.M. Since this was an Oklahoma midsummer, the sun was still high enough in the sky to make visibility perfectly clear. The ill-fated train consisted of motor 219 and trailer 239 as the first section, with car 224 as the second section. After a normal run northward on trackage paralleling the Santa Fe mainline, car 219 and trailer 239 pulled to a stop on the ORC mainline 205 feet north of the Berry station to await a southbound car, scheduled to take the siding at that point.

Mismatch of motor and trailer is evident from "down under" shot of motor 404 and trailer 402 on the North Canadian River bridge on May 4, 1946.
Ken Kidder

No one was aware of anything unusual until some shocked sailors in the rear of car 239 looked back to see car 224 bearing down on them at 30 miles per hour. Warned by the shouting sailors, passengers cleared the rear end of the trailer before car 224 crashed into their car. The force of the impact moved both car 219 and its trailer northward some 40 feet; the equipment of both trains was derailed and stopped in line with the track.

Rescuers found the rear of the trailer and the front of car 224 badly telescoped; the front end of trailer 239 was crushed inward seven feet; the rear end 13 feet. The front end of motor 224 was crushed inward 16 feet—the fatalities and most of the injuries occurred in this car. The employee killed was the motorman of car 224.

After decades of operation as a sleepy country interurban, the Norman line had been thrust into an unaccustomed role as a big city rapid transit line. It is a tribute to the skill and dedication of the Oklahoma Railway crews that this was the only incident to blemish an otherwise excellent safety and performance record set during the World War II years.

But while wartime passenger business set new records, ORC's freight operations were in trouble. In September 1942, the company had, over the objection of merchants, filed to abandon all rail express operations. The Oklahoma Corporation Commission the following year approved abandonment of heavy express service but the ORC was required to maintain its package express.

Sometime during the war, the company made either a conscious or unconscious decision to abandon all rail operations. The first major step was to sell the Oklahoma City belt lines to the Santa Fe and Rock Island railroads for $525,000. This occurred on August 15, 1944, after shippers along the Guthrie and El Reno lines had received assurances that the Santa Fe could use ORC lines to perform essential freight movements. The belt lines were soon de-electrified, and the Santa Fe and Rock Island substituted diesel locomotives.

Passenger increases, meanwhile, were spectacular. In 1944 city cars carried 52,102,512 passengers while the interurbans moved 2,278,126 commuters. City passengers could buy four tokens for a quarter with unlimited transfer privileges on streetcars and buses. The interurban fare to Norman was 44 cents or 77 cents for a round trip, El Reno passengers paid 66 cents or $1.20 for a round trip, and a ride north to Guthrie cost 72 cents or $1.30 for a round trip.

The U.S. victory over Japan in August 1945 brought forth a tremendous celebration in downtown Oklahoma City, as it did nearly everywhere in the U.S. Thousands snake-danced up and down the streets in exuberant celebration, tying up streetcar and interurban operation for hours on end. It was symbolic of what was to happen to the ORC in the months ahead.

Abruptly, the two naval bases at Norman closed down most operations just as gasoline for private cars became more plentiful. Industries laid off workers, and on the Norman division car miles nosedived by nearly one-half, from 78,000 miles in September 1945 to 42,000 miles in May 1946. Passenger revenue fell from $48,000 to $20,000 on the Norman line in the same period.

The beginning of the end for ORC's rail operations occurred in the fall of 1945 when the operators of the Oklahoma Transportation Co., a major Oklahoma intercity bus line, bought the assets of the Oklahoma Railway Co. and reorganized the company. Principals of the new management were Eugene Jordan and Robert S. Bowers. Proceeds from the sale of the freight operations, later disposal of the downtown terminal, and other real estate, put the firm back into solvency and enabled the new owners to proceed with a near debt-free company.

Jordan and Bowers promptly petitioned the corporation commission for permission to abandon the three interurban lines and all remaining city streetcars. There was little opposition to all of this—save the proposal to close the Norman division. Nearly everybody in Norman, it seemed, from the president of the university on down, demanded retention of the interurban. Much to Jordan and Bowers' chagrin, there were even proposals to upgrade the line into a true rail rapid transit line.

Forrest D. Monahan, Jr., in his article on the Norman interurban in the book, *Railroads in Oklahoma*, Oklahoma Historical Society, 1977, described the alarmed reaction from Norman division boosters:

"The Norman Chamber of Commerce objected, the Norman city manager announced a public meeting, and the Moore Chamber of Commerce protested. American Legion posts in both towns objected, noting that their brother veterans returning to the University needed the interurban. Dr. George L. Cross, President of the University of Oklahoma, wrote a worried letter of protest to the Corporation Commission. He noted that hundreds of university students were already commuting from Oklahoma City, and that many more would be commuting in the fall of 1946 because the university did not have housing for the huge number of returning veterans. . . .

"A fervent outburst arose from the citizens who resided along South Shields; they wrote indignant letters to the Commission . . . the indignation became a storm in March, 1946, when the company removed some runs from non-rush hour periods leaving patrons with hourly service instead of half hourly. Thirty minute coverage still served rush hours. The reduction from 42 daily round trips to 29 was about a 30 per cent decrease. The reduction was in fact greater, because the company removed some multiple sections from the trains. . . .

"One citizen not too subtly reminded the Commission that the protestors were also voters. More letters came in including petitions with more than 2,000 names. The Commission, all of whose members were elective, was suddenly cautious. It lost enthusiasm for the Oklahoma Railway hearing scheduled for May, 1946. The final hearing was delayed for a year."

Meantime, an anxious ORC lost little time in closing down the other two interurban divisions. With OCC blessing, on Saturday, November 9, 1946, both the Guthrie and El Reno lines were abandoned, the last cars leaving the downtown Oklahoma City terminal in the wee hours of the morning. The ORC did not offer replacement bus service, although intercity bus lines served both cities from the capital.

Due to an inability to get delivery of replacement buses fast enough, scheduled curtailment of the five remaining city streetcar lines had to be postponed from 1946 to 1947.

The fate of the Norman line remained up in the air. Its patronage, while certainly not up to wartime levels, remained much higher than the Depression; in May 1946, passenger revenue of $20,000 was four times the level of 1940; car mileage was twice the 1940 figure. As the fall season arrived, ORC found, true to University President Cross' predictions, that it had to schedule two- and three-section trains to handle the crowds of commuting students.

The Oklahoma Railway also stubbed its toe in its choice for lobbyist and spokesman in the changeover from rails to buses. The company hired New York transit consultant Col. Marmion D. Mills, an outspoken proponent of rubber-tired transport, to supervise the battle. Mills quickly became a controversial figure, and became embroiled with angry commuters, politicians and the newspapers as almost daily headlines kept the fight raging.

Suddenly, the company withdrew the abandonment petition. Mills stopped making statements (he was soon off to San Francisco to begin a partially successful campaign to rid the City by the Golden Gate of its streetcars) and quiet prevailed. By April 1947, the last of the city streetcar lines had been converted to buses. But the Norman interurban cars were still rolling.

In September of 1947 the company made its move. The Oklahoma Transportation Co. (also owned by Jordan and Bowers) put on a new schedule of 39 round-trip bus runs to Norman, nearly duplicating the rail service. Inevitably, interurban riding fell off. Meanwhile an elaborate new plan for a highway system in and near Norman took attention away from the interurban and its tracks.

Suddenly, visions of new freeways altered the picture. In early September 1947, the Norman city government changed its tune completely and decided it wanted to put a street on the interurban right-of-way within the city limits. The *Norman Transcript* advocated that the entire rail line be converted into a four-lane highway. Thus, in a much stronger position, the company again petitioned for abandonment.

When organized opposition failed to appear at the OCC hearing of September 18, 1947, the Norman interurban's fate was sealed. Approval was quickly granted, and, on the night of September 27, 1947, car 227 (one of the ex-Rockford interurbans) made the last northbound trip from Norman to the Oklahoma City terminal.

The demise of Oklahoma's largest and most viable electric rail passenger operation presented an interesting "what might have been" situation. Both Norman and Oklahoma City continued to grow by leaps and bounds, as did Moore, the little town halfway between, until the whole distance became one built-up urban sprawl. If organized opposition to the abandonment had remained firm after 1947, and if the company could have found the money for a handful of PCC cars and some track upgrading, who knows. . . ?

Chances are, any new image for the one rail line would have dulled after a time, just as the City Bus Co., successor to ORC, declined from 214 buses in 1947 to about 60 in 1967, when operations had to be taken over by a public authority. After World War II, Oklahoma City never was an outstanding public transportation town, although there have been serious efforts in the late 1970s to improve service in the face of freeway congestion and $1 a gallon gasoline.

Two one-time independent streetcar operations in Oklahoma City are of note. The Oklahoma City Traction Co., chartered in June 1910, operated some five miles of track in Oklahoma's capital city, with five cars in service. This line was taken over in 1915 by the North Canadian Valley Railway. On January 1, 1917, this short line, down to 3.3 track miles, was absorbed into the Oklahoma Railway Co.

The other independent company was the Capital Traction Co., original operator of the East Lake Park line past the state Capitol. It had two of its own cars and was reportedly sold to ORC in 1933, though it may in fact have been owned by the larger system earlier.

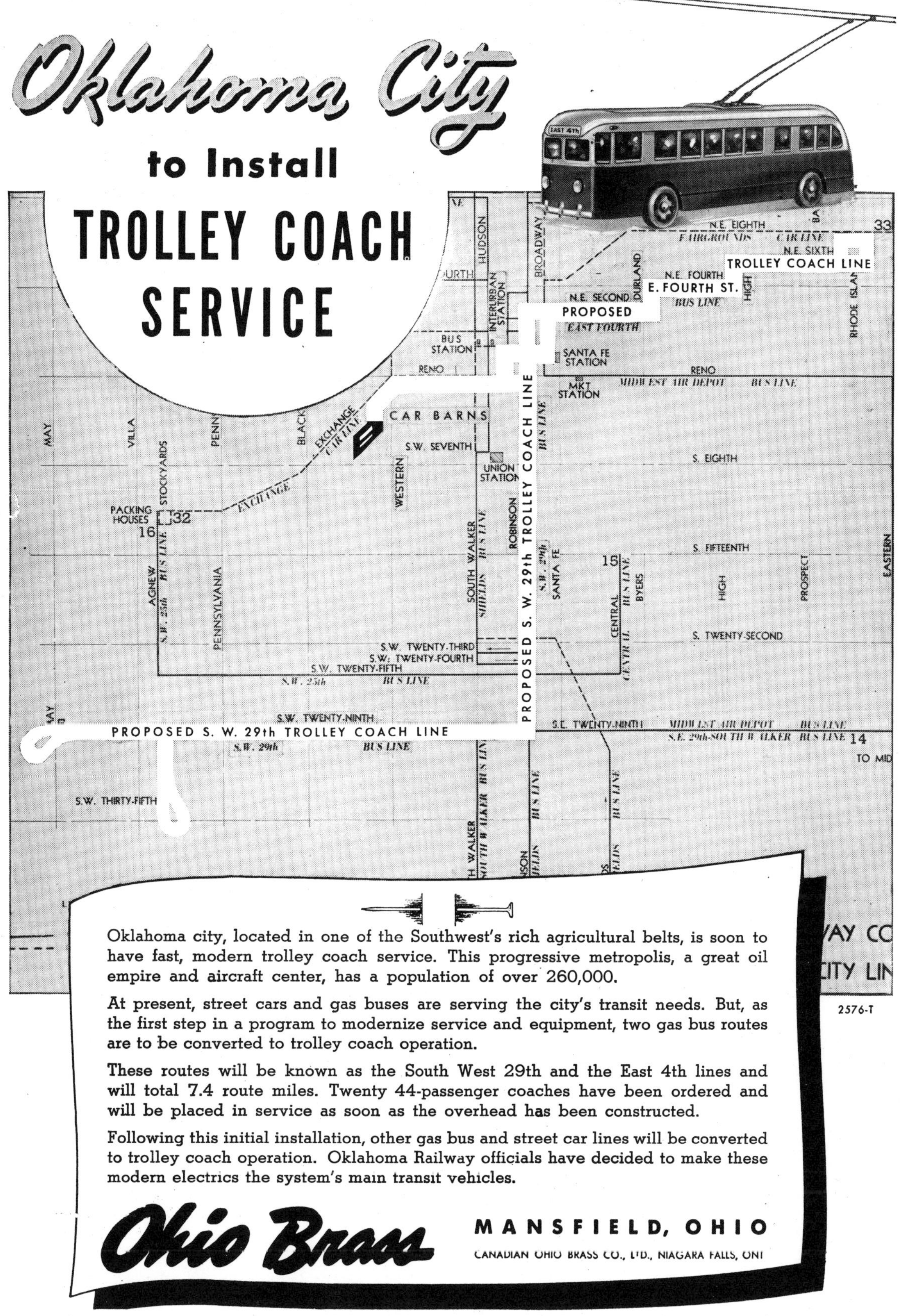

Oklahoma city, located in one of the Southwest's rich agricultural belts, is soon to have fast, modern trolley coach service. This progressive metropolis, a great oil empire and aircraft center, has a population of over 260,000.

At present, street cars and gas buses are serving the city's transit needs. But, as the first step in a program to modernize service and equipment, two gas bus routes are to be converted to trolley coach operation.

These routes will be known as the South West 29th and the East 4th lines and will total 7.4 route miles. Twenty 44-passenger coaches have been ordered and will be placed in service as soon as the overhead has been constructed.

Following this initial installation, other gas bus and street car lines will be converted to trolley coach operation. Oklahoma Railway officials have decided to make these modern electrics the system's main transit vehicles.

Ohio Brass   **MANSFIELD, OHIO**
CANADIAN OHIO BRASS CO., LTD., NIAGARA FALLS, ONT

What might have been: Management of Oklahoma Railway Co. briefly considered substitution of trolley coaches for streetcars. Ohio Brass 1945 advertisement in industry bible *Mass Transportation* detailed proposal for linking East Fourth streetcar and S.W. 29th bus line into new TC route. But electric buses never got beyond the talking stage, and no city in Oklahoma ever had them.

Magna Collection

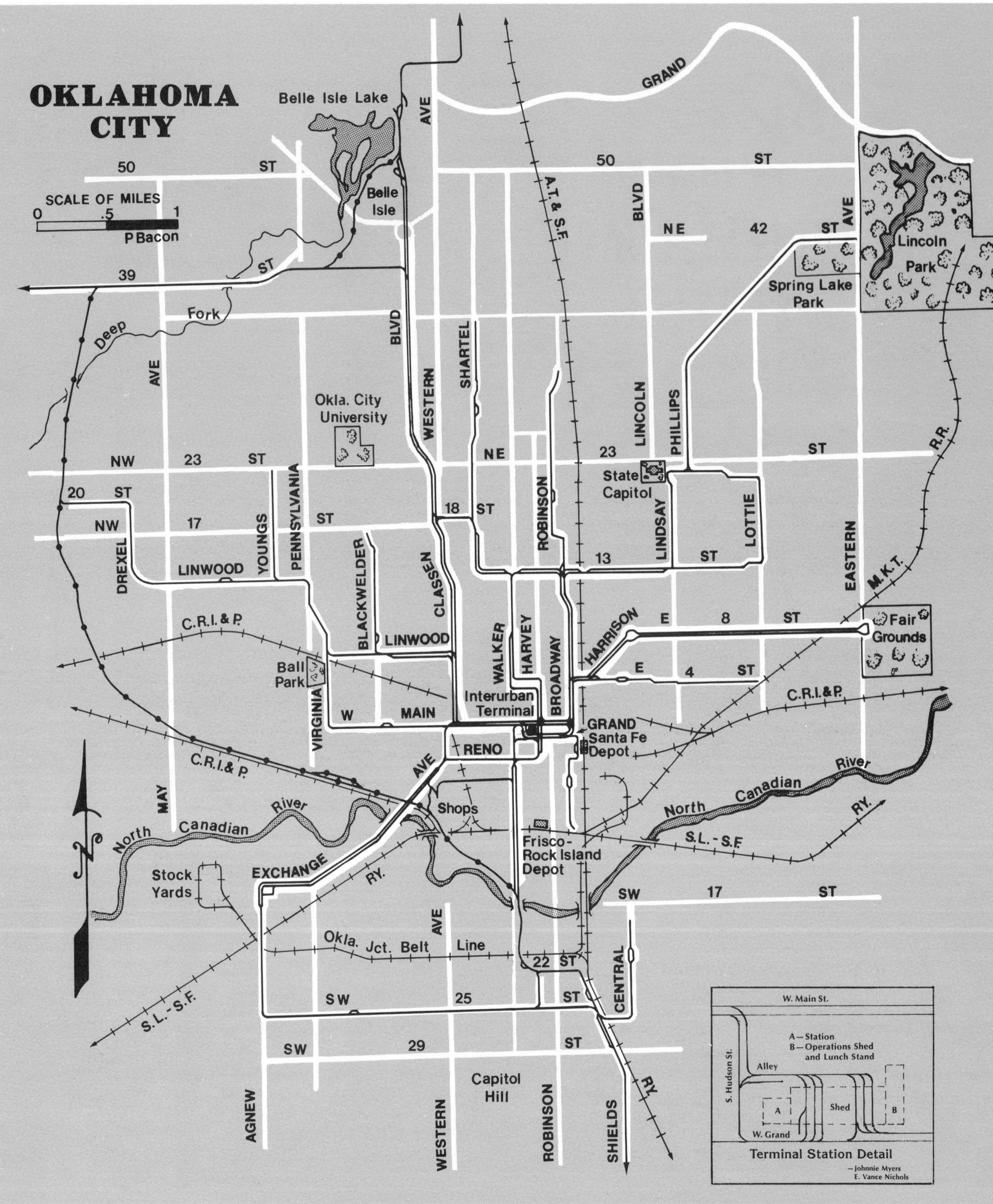
OKLAHOMA CITY
Belle Isle Lake
Belle Isle
SCALE OF MILES
0 .5 1
P Bacon
50 ST
39 ST
Deep Fork
GRAND
50 ST
BLVD
NE
42 ST
AVE
Lincoln Park
Spring Lake Park
A.T. & S.F.
AVE
BLVD
WESTERN
SHARTEL
NE
Okla. City University
NW 23 ST
20 ST
NW
17
DREXEL
LINWOOD
PENNSYLVANIA
YOUNGS
ST
AVE
23 ST
18 ST
NE ST
ROBINSON
State Capitol
23
13
LINCOLN
PHILLIPS
LINDSAY
LOTTIE
ST
ST
ST
EASTERN
R.R.
M.K.T.
BLACKWELDER
LINWOOD
CLASSEN
WALKER
HARVEY
BROADWAY
HARRISON
E 8 ST
E 4 ST
Fair Grounds
C.R.I. & P.
Ball Park
VIRGINIA
W MAIN
Interurban Terminal
RENO
GRAND
Santa Fe Depot
C.R.I. & P.
Shops
North Canadian River
Frisco-Rock Island Depot
S.L.-S.F.
RY.
MAY
North Canadian River
EXCHANGE
RY.
AVE
Stock Yards
Okla. Jct. Belt Line
SW 17 ST
22 ST
SW 25 ST
CENTRAL
SW 29 ST
ST
AGNEW
WESTERN
Capitol Hill
ROBINSON
SHIELDS
RY.
S.L.-S.F.
W. Main St.
A—Station
B—Operations Shed and Lunch Stand
S. Hudson St.
Alley
A
Shed
B
W. Grand
Terminal Station Detail
—Johnnie Myers
E. Vance Nichols
LEGEND
OKLA. RY. PASSENGER/OR FREIGHT
OKLA. RY. FREIGHT ONLY
STEAM RAILWAY

Early Days

LEFT: Early view of the downtown streetcar and interurban terminal, circa 1911. Layout was revised several times over the years, but the structure served until 1947.
Texas ERA Collection

MIDDLE: Northern Park was an early-day traction attraction in Oklahoma City; Traction Co. cars 6 and 5 served the park in 1911 when photo was taken.
Texas ERA Collection

BOTTOM: This was Delmar Gardens, another of Oklahoma City's early-day amusement centers.
Texas ERA Collection

TOP: Builders photo of ORC car 59, whose deep windows let plenty of Oklahoma sunshine in.
Theodore P. Taetsch from Texas ERA Collection

BOTTOM: This type of heavy wooden car was used until arrival of the boomer lightweight interurbans.
Stephen D. Maguire Collection

City Streetcars

With one of the city's principal department stores in the background, city car 151 begins its trek out to Belle Isle, September 13, 1938. Car and sisters 152-153 were later used on the interurban lines. *William C. Janssen*

TOP: Dinkies were what some people called Oklahoma Railway's single-truck Birney safety cars. This one bobs and weaves its way over the 17th Street Loop, circa 1935.

Robert V. Mehlenbeck

MIDDLE: Nostalgic, to say the least, is the sight of gasoline selling for as low as fifteen and a half cents a gallon. Here is single-ender 149, one of the ex-Michigan cars, heading for Belle Isle in 1939.

Magna Collection

RIGHT: One of the few pre-lightweight holdovers in the ORC city car fleet was arch-roof car 73, shown on Main Street downtown, 1941.

Railway Negative Exchange

LEFT: "Shorty" lightweight cars, seating only 36 passengers but riding on double trucks, ruled some of the lighter Oklahoma City lines. A pair of these cars passes on a short stretch of double track on South 22nd near the Canadian River bridge. They are working the South Shields line on trackage shared with the Norman interurban.
Robert V. Mehlenbeck

MIDDLE: Single-track Linwood line drew some of the smaller double-ended cars. Here is the 124, out on Drexel in 1946.　　*Charles Smallwood*

BOTTOM: Skirvin Tower and its WKY radio studios form the backdrop for one of the 1930-built single-end city cars, circa 1946.
Interurbans

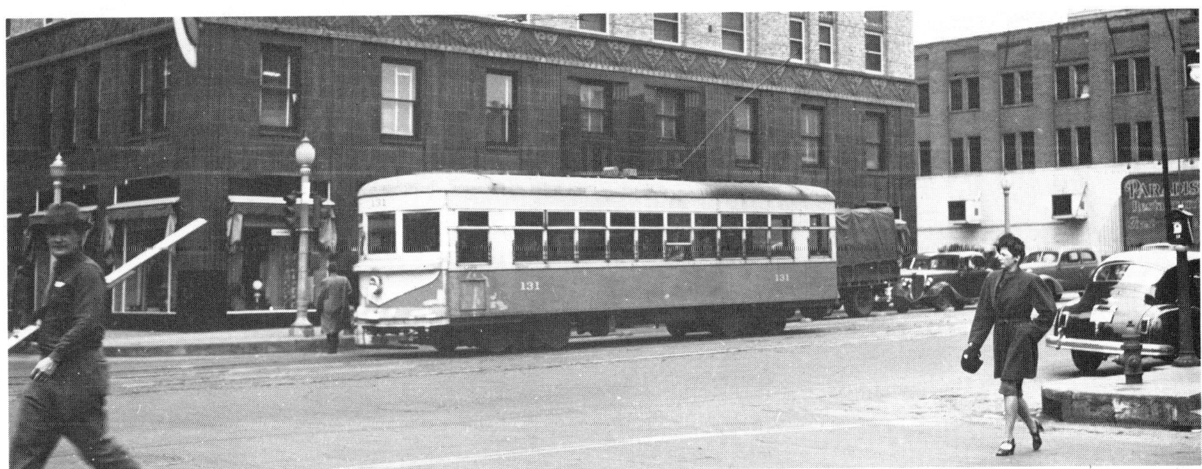

City Car Varieties

Belle Isle car heads north on the Classen Blvd. neutral ground, in June of 1934. Photographer Robert Mehlenbeck took this and other Oklahoma City photos during a two-month visit, the purpose of which was to assist his father in building a home for his oldest sister and her family.
Robert V. Mehlenbeck

Grass was not as high as an elephant's eye, but nevertheless flourishing on and about the right-of-way near the Canadian River bridge. Here, Shields Blvd. car 117 leaves the freight belt line and prepares to cross the river, June 1934.
Robert V. Mehlenbeck

Coming off the Canadian River bridge and onto South Walker is Central car 68, heading for the business district in June 1934.
Robert V. Mehlenbeck

TOP: Inside-hung lightweight trucks are shown clearly in this photo of car 133. It's May of 1934, and Warner Baxter is playing in *Stand Up and Cheer* at the Midwest Theater. Despite the Depression, Oklahoma Railway kept its cars spic and span.
Robert V. Mehlenbeck

BOTTOM: Linwood car 121 pauses for traffic to clear leaving the downtown depot. If you look closely to the left, you can see an Oklahoma Railways tower car turning the corner onto Main Street in front of the Hightower Building.
Robert V. Mehlenbeck

Variety was the spice of life, and of Oklahoma Railway's city car fleet. Many types were represented (see roster). In May and June of 1934 Robert Mehlenbeck roamed the Exchange Ave. shops and the shots on the two pages of cars 66, 67, 87 and 106 are but a few captured by his camera.

Robert V. Mehlenbeck

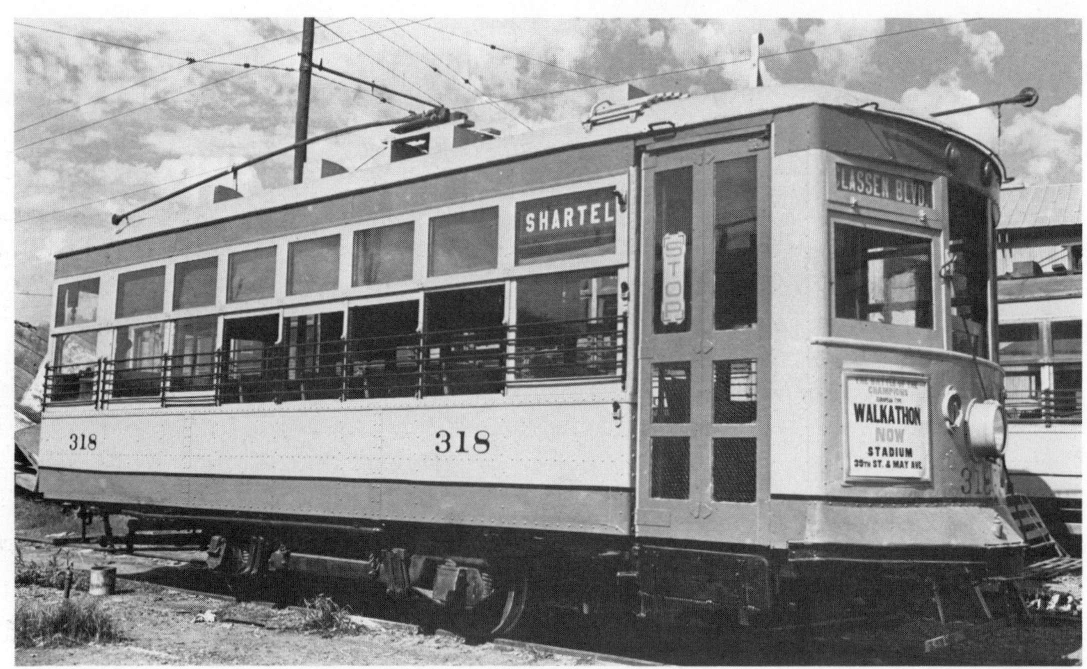

ABOVE AND RIGHT: Even the ubiquitous single-truck Birney came in many variations. Both cars 318 and 323 were on the Oklahoma City roster. The Shartel and 17th Street Loop rail lines were early victims of bus substitution in the Sooner State's largest city. *Robert V. Mehlenbeck*

BELOW: Seventeenth Street Station was the first major interchange stop north of the central terminal for El Reno, Guthrie interurbans as well as Belle Isle city cars. Here are city cars 118 and 145 pausing in an April 1947 rainstorm. *John B. Fink Collection from Charles Winters*

Boomers

In railroad parlance, a "boomer" is an employe who emigrates from one line to another. Car 221, with its high steps and well-worn look, was a boomer too, coming to the rescue of war-time Oklahoma commuters from a line in Ohio and Indiana. No doubt the young sailors based at Norman had little trouble bounding up those steps, but how about grandma with an armload of packages?
Interurbans

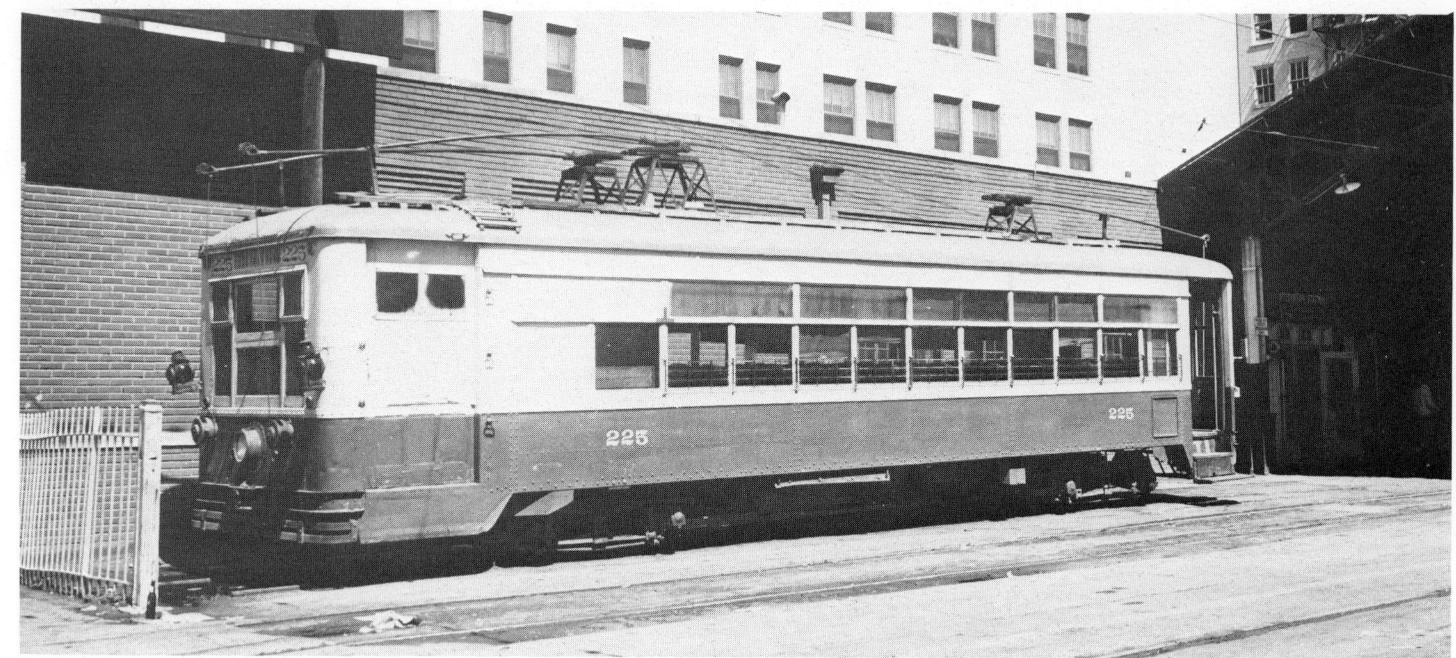

Pocket track at the downtown Oklahoma City terminal often held some of ORC's more interesting hand-me-down interurbans. Photo of car 225, purchased second-hand in 1937 from the Rockford, Ill., interurban system, spotlights car's unique "automotive" rear end (equipped with headlight for backup moves), twin rear trolley poles and front pole, also for backup moves. Car 234, with its round quarter windows, was scrounged for Oklahoma Railway by the U.S. Navy during World War II from Ohio's Dayton-Xenia Railway. Note sign overhead advertising "Cars for Norman Naval Bases."

Both: Magna Collection

TOP: Here's a character study of car 222 at the Oklahoma City terminal.
Interurbans

MIDDLE: A sunny Sunday in 1938 finds ORC car 229 near the end of the line in El Reno. This car had been acquired from Rockford, Ill., the preceding year.
Robert W. Richardson,

RIGHT: Formerly of the Dayton-Xenia interurban in Ohio, ORC car 232 leaves downtown Oklahoma City for the Classen Blvd. right-of-way, 1944.
Robert W. Richardson,
Laurence Veysey Collection

RIGHT: Closing out a second interurban career, Oklahoma Railway car 221 rumbles down South Walker, the Oklahoma City terminal a few blocks behind, on its way to Norman in 1946. ORC had picked this car up from the old Fort Wayne & Lima line, back in Indiana/Ohio. Poor track paving gave hint that the end of operations was not far off.

Charles Smallwood

BELOW: Another boomer trolley in Soonerland was ex-Flint, Mich., car 149, shown on May 1, 1946, at the Belle Isle loop ready for the return journey downtown and out to the Capitol. *Charles Smallwood*

Downtown Terminal

TOP: Canopied train shed at the Oklahoma City interurban station was a busy place back on September 24, 1935. City cars loaded at right, buses and interurbans at left. *Robert V. Mehlenbeck*

BOTTOM: Tinker Field service was provided by bus, one of which loads at left at the downtown Oklahoma City interurban terminal on July 1, 1945. Norman train awaits highball on track at right. Tinker Army Air Base was a World War II development, and was built several miles from the nearest interurban. *William C. Janssen*

In front of the terminal, car 217 pushes out for Norman on May 15, 1934. Car was painted grey with red trim.
Robert V. Mehlenbeck

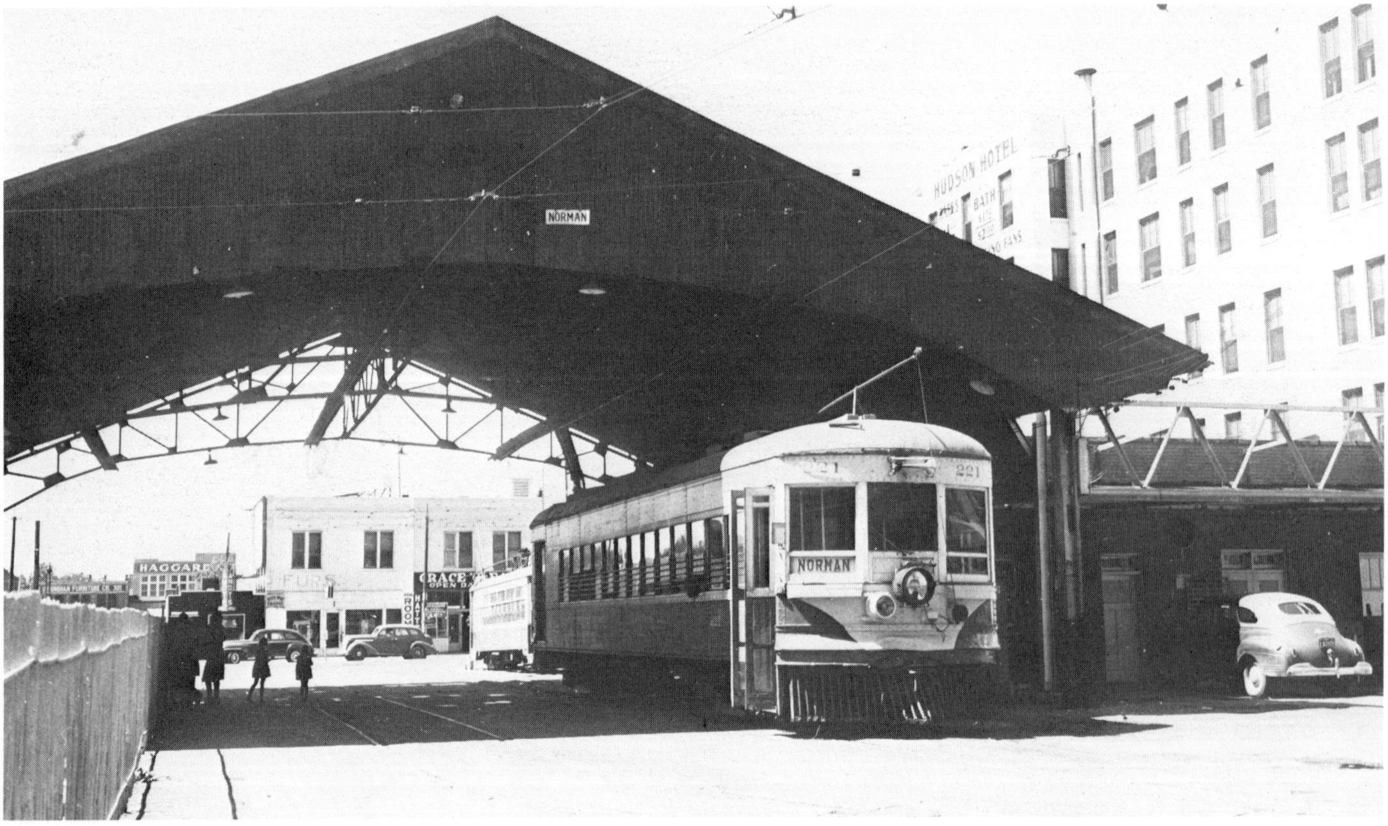

Here's the rear of the terminal on a quiet day, perhaps a Sunday. By 1946, only two tracks, plus a one-car pocket track, were available for rail passenger loading.
Interurbans

Wartime

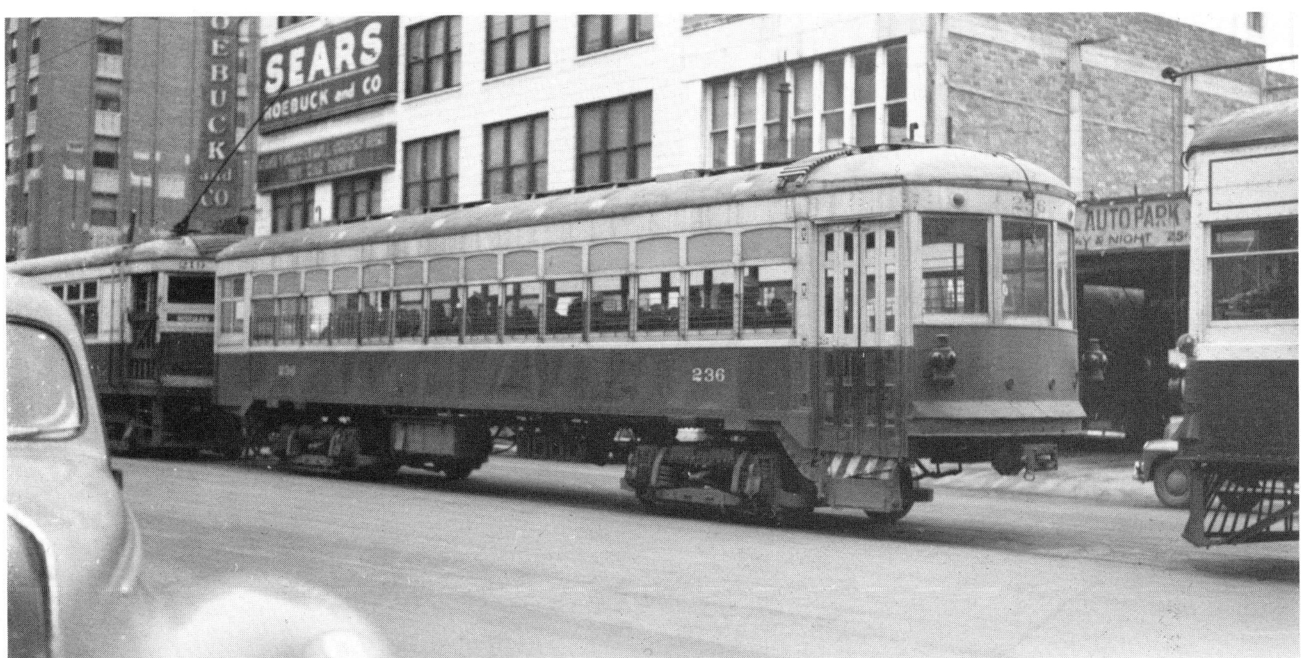

TOP: Wartime crowds descended on the Oklahoma Railway Co., filling the streets once again with streetcars. Trailer operation became common, especially on the Norman division, as witness this wartime scene spotlighting ex-Schenectady trailer 236 being pulled by motor 219.
Mark Effle Collection

BOTTOM: Patriotic slogans were carried on sides of interurbans during World War II. Here is 234 in the pocket track at the Oklahoma City intcrurban tcrminal on July 1, 1945. Sign above car emphasizes service to Norman naval bases, which did account for king-size share of the company's rail traffic in those days.
William C. Janssen

RIGHT: Quaint—perhaps even ugly—would describe ORC's 400 series, which were freight cars converted into passenger cars to handle wartime traffic. Here is motor 401 and trailer laying over at Norman in 1944.   *Interurbans*

BELOW: Closeup of one of the 400-series cars. Original drop-center passenger car configuration is obvious. Then car was converted into a freight motor, finally back into passenger car to cope with crush crowds during the war.   *Interurbans*

BOTTOM: Trailer 402, a box on wheels, shows to what lengths Oklahoma Railway went during the war to put passengers into anything that would roll.
William C. Janssen

Norman Line

Speedy private right-of-way into Oklahoma City for Norman cars included trestle over the North Canadian River. Here is car 221 crossing it on July 1, 1945.
William C. Janssen

Norman line ended in a loop not far from the center of the city and the University of Oklahoma. Here is a 1946 double-header about to depart for "The City." Cars are from the ex-Rockford, Ill., group.
Interurbans

NORMAN DIVISION—Daily except as noted

	Mls	A.M	A.M	A.M	A.M	A.M	A.M	A.M	P.M	P.M	P.M	P.M	P.M	P.M	P.M	P.M	P.M	P.M	P.M	P.M	A.M
Lv. Okla. City Terminal Sta.	0	*5:03	6:03	7:03	8:03	9:03	10:03	11:03	12:03	1:03	2:03	3:03	4:03	5:03	6:03	7:03	8:03	9:03	10:03	11:03	12:03
Moore	9	5:29	6:29	7:29	8:29	9:29	10:29	11:29	12:29	1:29	2:29	3:29	4:29	5:29	6:29	7:29	8:29	9:29	10:29	11:29	12:29
Ar. Norman	18	5:43	6:43	7:43	8:43	9:43	10:43	11:43	12:43	1:43	2:43	3:43	4:43	5:43	6:43	7:43	8:43	9:43	10:43	11:43	12:43
		A.M	A.M	A.M	A.M	A.M	A.M	A.M	P.M	P.M	P.M	P.M	P.M	P.M	P.M	P.M	P.M	P.M	P.M	P.M	A.M

*Daily Except Sunday

	Mls	A.M	A.M	A.M	A.M	A.M	A.M	A.M	P.M	P.M	P.M	P.M	P.M	P.M	P.M	P.M	P.M	P.M	P.M	P.M	A.M
Lv. Norman		*5:47	6:47	7:47	8:47	9:47	10:47	11:47	12:47	1:47	2:47	3:47	4:47	5:47	6:47	7:47	8:47	9:47	10:47	11:47	12:47
Moore		6:03	7:03	8:03	9:03	10:03	11:03	12:03	1:03	2:03	3:03	4:03	5:03	6:03	7:03	8:03	9:03	10:03	11:03	12:03	1:03
Ar. Okla. City		[illegible]	[illegible]	[illegible]	[illegible]	10:27	11:27	12:27	1:27	2:27	3:27	4:27	5:27	6:27	7:27	8:27	9:27	10:27	11:27	12:27	1:27
		A.M	P.M	P.M	P.M	P.M	P.M	P.M	P.M	P.M	P.M	P.M	P.M	P.M	P.M	P.M	P.M	P.M	P.M	A.M	A.M

... Oklahoma Railway public timetable. A decade later the ...ourly with many extra sections.

ABOVE: Taking siding for Norman car 221 (right) is interurban 223 (left). These are two of the ex-Fort Wayne-Lima cars.
William C. Janssen

RIGHT: Car 222 has just left the Norman terminal, and is picking up speed toward "The City." It is July 1, 1945, and servicemen still predominate among the riders.
W. C. Janssen

> Rode on cars 221 + 222 when at O.U.

Flying green flags for a following section, Oklahoma Railway interurban car 404 and ex-Schenectady, N.Y., trailer 236 rocket into Norman, Okla., on July 1, 1945, after a fast run from Oklahoma City. So desperate was the company for passenger seats during World War II that it converted freight cars, including 404, into passenger cars.

William C. Janssen

---The Oklahoma Daily
October 19, 1946
(Norman, Oklahoma)

WARNING

to Citizens of Norman

Do you know that the Oklahoma Railway Company is attempting to abandon the Norman Interurban Line? That the Matter has been set for hearing on October 22 before the Corporation Commission at Oklahoma City?

Do you realize that:

(1) This will be a step backward in the progress of Norman in losing this one sure, fast means of transportation to Oklahoma City.

(2) That hundreds of students, who have to commute to Norman on this line, would either find it impossible to attend school or their chances of getting back and forth every day on them would be greatly lessened if this interurban is abandoned.

(3) the housewives, who shop in Oklahoma City, realize that there is no place on busses to carry their packages and bundles, as there is on interurban cars.

(4) Do you realize that the underpass on the highway to Oklahoma City becomes flooded, interrupting speedy service.

(5) That the interurban offers the safest, most economical and speedy means of getting back and forth from Oklahoma City.

(6) That business men in Norman, who depend on the fast service for perishable commodities. will suffer a loss in business efficiency.

(7) That School Districts along this right of way will lose a considerable amount of revenue, which will increase the tax burden on the people in the District.

You should immediately call your City Manager and Chamber of Commerce to protest this and if possible, appear October 22 before the Corporation Commission.

(J. G. DICKINSON)

LEFT: 1946 fight to preserve Norman interurbans was a bitter one. This advertisement appeared in the University of Oklahoma Daily on October 19 of that year. Public outcry against abandonment was successful, if only briefly.
Magna Collection from J.G. Dickinson

BELOW: High-stepping interurban 217 kicks up dust on its northbound run from Norman near 56th and South Shields, Oklahoma City, May 26, 1934.
Robert V. Mehlenbeck

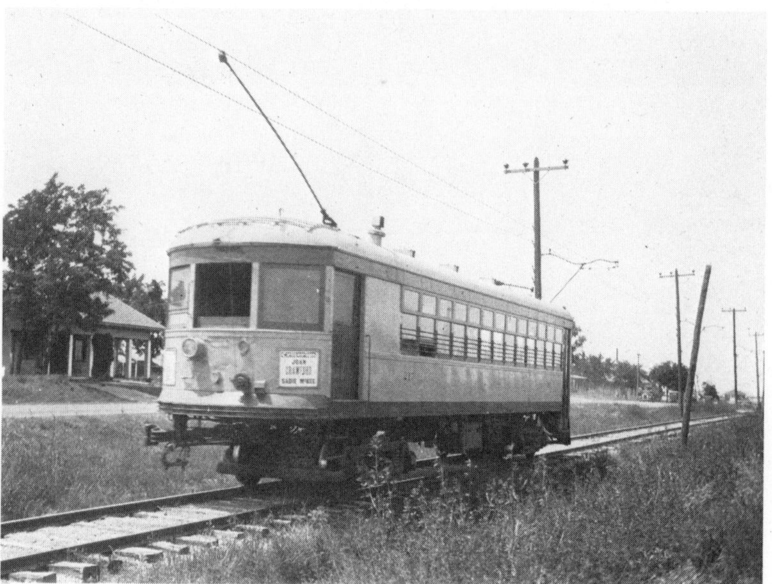

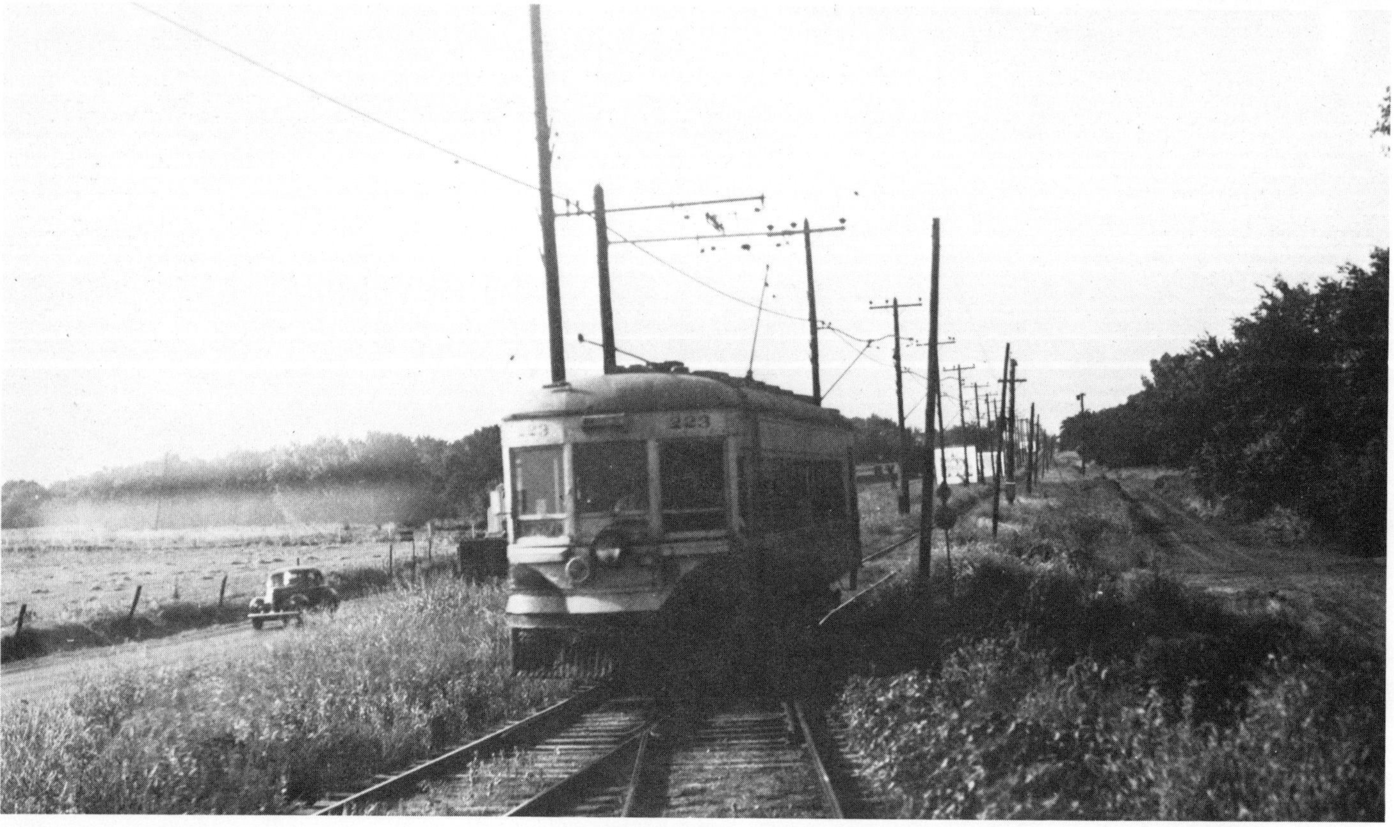

Mowing the weeds between the rails as it flies, Oklahoma Railway interurban 223, one of the ex-Fort Wayne-Lima cars, speeds towards Norman, 1946.
Charles Smallwood

TOP: Big-time railroading meant trains, and Oklahoma Railway had them on the Norman line. This two-car schedule included motor 218 and trailer 235 and has paused on July 1, 1945, on South Shields to let a northbound car pass (blur at right). *William C. Janssen*

INSERT: Heavy riding turned the Norman line into real rapid transit. This 1946 scene shows Niles motor 404 and trailer 402 on the North Canadian River bridge. *Ken Kidder*

BOTTOM: Turning onto Grand from South Walker, this two-car Norman train will tie up at the central terminal in a matter of a minute or two. New 1946 Ford, plus two bus stations in view, signify that the end of rail operations cannot be far away. *Interurbans*

Freight

Three of ORC's freight locomotives were available for service to handle terminal switching in the Oklahoma City area, before freight operations were sold off during World War II. Loco 600 was photographed in 1937 at Oklahoma City; the 601 was taken in 1944, and the 602 at the Exchange Shops near the end of operations. *Edwin Keane;*
Carl Blaubach; Texas ERA Collection

Line Cars

TOP: Aging wooden line car 500 adjusts the overhead trolley wire at N.W. 13th and Broadway Place, December 30, 1940. Motorized tower truck works behind.
John B. Fink Collection
from Charles Winters

MIDDLE: Peeling paint did not keep ORC line car from its appointed rounds.
Magna Collection

RIGHT: 1915-built city car was converted to work car service, but retained snazzy paint scheme. It is shown here at the Exchange shops, 1945.   *Interurbans*

Retired

Gallery of once-proud interurbans retired to the Exchange Ave. shops backyard in 1934. Car 201 (above) with off-center headlight in weathered tan and cream paint job; (left) an interior shot of the same car—note plain wooden board floor and "warning of danger" sign under the two Ohmer fare registers. One registered city fares, the other interurban. Facing page, top photo shows car 203, its paint badly peeling, coupled to ex-New York City elevated car which the company acquired for trailer duty. Closeup of elevated car is on facing page, center. Car 212 is shown with wooden pilot, probably not in active service.

All: Robert V. Mehlenbeck

The End

TOP: After close of service in 1946, city cars, and some interurbans, were put out to pasture at the Exchange Shops. Norman cars, still in service, continued to use the facility. *Interurbans*

BOTTOM: Only six days before the end of service, car 227 loads on the loop at the Norman terminal for the return journey to downtown Oklahoma City. Oklahoma Transportation Co. buses were already providing a frequent service, and this shiny motor coach seems to be getting the passengers today. Within a week, Oklahoma Railway streetcars and interurbans would be only a memory. *Interurbans from James A. Williams*

El Reno Interurban Railway

EL RENO, county seat town of Canadian County just west of Oklahoma City, originally possessed a two-mile streetcar line served by one gasoline-powered railcar. By December 1908 the El Reno Interurban Railway Co. was officially in existence, capitalized at one million dollars, and the city line was electrified.

What the new company's promoters really had in mind was a 30-mile interurban, to connect El Reno, an important division point on the Rock Island Railroad, with Oklahoma City via Yukon, an intermediate town with grain elevators and flour mills. A September 8, 1908, report that the Oklahoma Railway Co. of Oklahoma City was about to take over the El Reno company was stoutly denied.

However, on August 1, 1911, the ORC did acquire the line and equipment of the El Reno Interurban Co. and the city lines in El Reno.

On Sunday, December 3, 1911, the Oklahoma Railway Co. began running interurbans on regular schedule between Oklahoma City and El Reno. Cars left the Southern Hotel in downtown El Reno every hour from 6:00 A.M. until 11:00 P.M. Streetcars in the city of El Reno were running every half hour, leaving the Southern Hotel at 10 minutes until and 20 minutes after the hour.

With its acquisition by Oklahoma Railway Co., the El Reno Interurban Railway Co. quickly lost its identity and became a part of the vast ORC trolley empire. Date of the ORC termination of in-town trolley operation in El Reno is uncertain, but the interurbans were still running into that town in February 1946 when Oklahoma Railway Co. petitioned the state corporation commission for abandonment of that segment of its system. The commission granted the request in late October and on Saturday, November 9, 1946, the big red-and-cream ORC trolleys made their last runs into El Reno.

This beauty of an interurban car did not carry El Reno Interurban on letterboard for long, since line was absorbed into ORC at a very early date.
Magna Collection

TOP: Jewett built El Reno Interurban car 1, shown at the University Station, Oklahoma City, on way to El Reno.
Texas ERA Collection from E. Harper Charlton

BOTTOM: Local service in El Reno disappeared relatively early, but here is an Oklahoma Railway car in service, circa 1920.
Stephen D. Maguire Collection

EL RENO DIVISION—Daily except as noted.

	Mls	A.M	A.M	A.M	A.M	A.M	A.M	A.M	P.M	P.M	P.M	P.M	P.M	P.M	P.M	P.M	P.M	P.M	P.M
Lv. Okla. City Terminal Station	0	*5:15	6:15	7:30	8:30	9:30	10:30	11:30	12:30	1:30	2:30	3:30	4:30	5:30	6:30	7:30	9:05	10:05	11:30
17tn Street Station	2	5:24	6:24	7:39	8:39	9:39	10:39	11:39	12:39	1:39	2:39	3:39	3:49	5:39	6:39	7:39	9:14	10:14	11:39
40th Street Station	4	5:30	6:30	7:45	8:45	9:45	10:45	11:45	12:45	1:45	2:45	3:45	4:45	5:45	6:45	7:45	9:20	10:20	11:45
Bethany	9	5:41	6:41	:756	9:00	9:58	10:58	11:58	12:58	1:58	3:00	4:00	5:00	6:00	7:00	7:58	9:32	10:32	11:57
Yukon	16	6:00	7:00	8:15	9:15	10:15	11:15	12:15	1:15	2:15	3:17	4:17	5:17	6:17	7:16	8:15	9:50	10:49	12:15
Banner	23	6:10	7:10	8:27	9:27	10:27	11:27	12:27	1:27	2:27	3:30	4:30	5:30	6:30	7:29	8:27	10:02	11:02	12:27
Ar. El Reno	29	6:27	7:27	8:46	9:46	10:46	11:46	12:46	1:46	2:46	3:50	4:50	5:50	6:50	7:49	8:47	10:21	11:21	12:46
		A.M	A.M	A.M	A.M	A.M	A.M	P.M	P.M	P.M	P.M	P.M	P.M	P.M	P.M	P.M	P.M	P.M	A.M

*Daily Except Sunday

	Mls	A.M	A.M	A.M	A.M	A.M	A.M	P.M	P.M	P.M	P.M	P.M	P.M	P.M	P.M	P.M	P.M	P.M	P.M
Lv. El Reno		*5:30	6:30	7:30	9:02	10:02	11:02	12:02	1:02	2:02	3:00	4:00	5:00	6:00	7:15	8:12	9:20	10:30	11:45
Banner		5:47	6:47	7:47	9:20	10:20	11:20	12:20	1:20	2:20	3:18	4:18	5:18	6:18	7:33	8:31	9:38	10:48	12:03
Yukon		5:59	6:59	7:59	9:34	10:34	11:34	12:34	1:34	2:34	3:32	4:32	5:32	6:32	7:45	8:43	9:50	11:00	12:15
Bethany		6:14	7:14	8:14	9:48	10:48	11:48	12:48	1:48	2:48	3:47	4:47	5:47	6:47	8:00	8:56	10:03	11:13	12:28
40th Street Station		6:28	7:28	8:28	10:02	11:02	12:02	1:02	2:02	3:02	4:02	5:02	6:02	7:02	8:14	9:10	10:18	11:28	12:43
17th Street Station		6:34	7:34	8:34	10:07	11:07	12:07	1:07	2:07	3:07	4:07	5:07	6:07	7:07	8:19	9:15	10:23	11:33	12:48
Ar. Okla. City Terminal Station		6:45	7:45	8:45	10:17	11:17	12:17	1:17	2:17	3:17	4:17	5:17	6:17	7:17	8:29	9:25	10:33	11:43	12:58
		A.M	A.M	A.M	A.M	A.M	P.M	P.M	P.M	P.M	P.M	P.M	P.M	P.M	P.M	P.M	P.M	P.M	A.M

*Daily Except Sunday

From the June 20, 1930, Oklahoma Railway public timetable.

Turning onto Main Street from Hudson, car 229 starts out for El Reno, circa 1938.   *William C. Janssen*

TOP: Nineteen thirties were lean years for Oklahoma Railway, which explains why the rails and ties of the El Reno interurban didn't have the luxury of ballast. El Reno-bound 225 meets car 219 on September 13, 1938.
William C. Janssen

MIDDLE: Fresh eggs, poultry of any kind were always available at the White Turkey Ranch, just under the interurban trestle just now feeling the weight of an El Reno-bound car, 1940. *Magna Collection*

RIGHT: Bethany was important intermediate stop on the El Reno interurban, even back in 1940 before the town grew into a major Oklahoma City bedroom community. *Magna Collection*

Guthrie Railway Company

BEFITTING its status as the early capital of Oklahoma Territory, Guthrie boasted one of the earliest electric streetcar operations in Soonerland. The Logan County seat town in North Central Oklahoma was awarded a street railway franchise as early as May 1903.

The Guthrie Railway Co. was incorporated in January 1905, capitalized at $600,000. On May 26 of that year the *Guthrie Daily Leader* ran a page one headline entitled "Trolley Begins to Sing" and reported the first electric streetcar had appeared on city streets at 10:30 o'clock that morning. Thus the town of Guthrie became a pioneer in Oklahoma electric traction, with only McAlester, Muskogee and Oklahoma City enjoying trolley cars previous to that date.

Power for the 6.5-mile Guthrie trolley line was purchased from the Guthrie Light & Power Co. and there were nine cars in service. Tracks reached Highland Park, Island Park and Guthrie Park. Guthrie's 1908 population, soon after statehood, totaled 13,808 residents. Alas, despite its improved local transportation, Guthrie lost the state capital to Oklahoma City.

In the 1910s the expanding Oklahoma Railway Co. of Oklahoma City evidenced interest in connecting with Guthrie and on July 20, 1916, interurban cars began making runs from downtown Guthrie the 31 miles south into Oklahoma City's streetcar terminal. Guthrie's population that year had declined to 11,654. It was at this time that the Guthrie Railway Co. came under control of the ORC, but it kept its separate identity for several years.

The local streetcar operation was a victim of the Great Depression but the interurban to Oklahoma City continued, albeit with reduced service. In February 1946 the Oklahoma Railway Co. petitioned the Oklahoma Corporation Commission to abandon its line from Oklahoma City to Guthrie.

By this time, motor transport was available. City buses were in operation, and Guthrie's School District No. 60 had just purchased five new buses to transport 200 rural pupils into city schools. Also by mid-1946 the Santa Fe Trailways had exhibited one of its brand new motor buses in downtown Guthrie. And, the G.A. Nichols Bus Co. was operating 18 daily buses from Oklahoma City north to Edmond (location of Central State College) and 14 daily buses on to Guthrie.

In late October 1946 the state corporation commission granted the ORC abandonment request and at midnight on Saturday, November 9, the last trolley car left Guthrie for Oklahoma City, terminating three decades of interurban service.

Construction of Guthrie Railway Company's mainline along Oklahoma Ave. is in progress in this 1905 photo, from an old postcard. View looks east. *Stephen D. Maguire Collection*

TOP: Lone electric car has the road to itself, circa 1906, in this Guthrie Railway Co. postcard view.
Railway Negative Exchange

BOTTOM: Builders photo of Guthrie Railway Co. car 4, 1905.   *Stephen D. Maguire Collection*

GUTHRIE DIVISION—Daily except as noted

	Mls	A.M	A.M	A.M	A.M	A.M	A.M	A.M	P.M	P.M	P.M	P.M	P.M	P.M	P.M	P.M	P.M	P.M	P.M	P.M
Lv. Okla. City Terminal Station	0	*5:30	6:30	7:35	8:35	9:35	10:35	11:35	12:35	1:35	2:35	3:35	4:35	5:35	6:35	7:35	8:35	9:35	10:35	11:35
17th Street Station	2	5:39	6:39	7:44	8:44	9:44	10:44	11:44	12:44	1:44	2:44	3:44	4:44	5:44	6:44	7:44	8:44	9:44	10:44	11:44
40th Street Station	4	5:44	6:44	7:49	8:49	9:49	10:49	11:49	12:49	1:49	2:49	3:49	4:49	5:49	6:49	7:49	8:49	9:49	10:49	11:49
Britton	8	5:54	6:54	7:59	8:59	9:59	10:59	11:59	12:59	1:59	2:59	3:59	4:59	5:59	6:59	7:59	8:59	9:59	10:59	11:59
Edmond	15	6:07	7:07	8:13	9:13	10:13	11:13	12:13	1:13	2:13	3:13	4:13	5:13	6:13	7:13	8:13	9:13	10:13	11:13	12:13
Ar. Guthrie	31	6:35	7:38	8:45	9:45	10:45	11:45	12:45	1:45	2:45	3:45	4:45	5:45	6:45	7:45	8:45	9:45	10:45	11:45	12:45
		A.M	A.M	A.M	A.M	A.M	A.M	P.M	P.M	P.M	P.M	P.M	P.M	P.M	P.M	P.M	P.M	P.M	P.M	A.M

* Daily Except Sunday

	Mls	A.M	A.M	A.M	A.M	A.M	A.M	A.M	P.M	P.M	P.M	P.M	P.M	P.M	P.M	P.M	P.M	P.M	P.M	P.M
Lv. Guthrie		*5:40	6:40	7:50	8:50	9:50	10:50	11:50	12:50	1:50	2:50	3:50	4:50	5:50	6:50	7:50	8:50	9:50	10:50	11:50
Edmond		6:10	7:10	8:22	9:22	10:22	11:22	12:22	1:22	2:22	3:22	4:22	5:22	6:22	7:22	8:22	9:22	10:22	11:22	12:22
Britton		6:24	7:24	8:35	9:35	10:35	11:35	12:35	1:35	1:35	3:35	4:35	5:35	6:35	7:35	8:35	9:35	10:35	11:35	12:35
40th Street Station		6:34	7:34	8:45	9:45	10:45	11:45	12:45	1:45	2:45	3:45	4:45	5:45	6:45	7:45	8:45	9:45	10:45	11:45	12:45
17th Street Station		6:40	7:40	8:50	9:50	10:50	11:50	12:50	1:50	2:50	3:50	4:50	5:50	6:50	7:50	8:50	9:50	10:50	11:50	12:50
Ar. Okla. City Terminal Station		6:50	7:50	9:00	10:00	11:00	12:00	1:00	2:00	3:00	4:00	5:00	6:00	7:00	8:00	9:00	10:00	11:00	12:00	1:00
		A.M	A.M	A.M	A.M	A.M	A.M	P.M	P.M	P.M	P.M	P.M	P.M	P.M	P.M	P.M	P.M	P.M	M.M	A.M

*Daily Except Sunday

From the June 20, 1930, Oklahoma Railway public timetable.

Arrival of the Oklahoma City interurban into Guthrie was over somewhat uneven track. Here is ex-Rockford interurban car 225 bowling past laid-up car 403 on short siding south of station. The date is September 12, 1938.

William C. Janssen

TOP: Ancient deck-roof city car 94 was sometimes pressed into service on the interurban lines. It sits on the interurban terminal pocket track ready for a run to Guthrie in May 1934. *Robert V. Mehlenbeck*

BOTTOM: On last leg of its journey from Guthrie, car 227 noses into Oklahoma City interurban terminal on a rainy September day, 1938. Hotel Black on corner was one of The City's better-known hostelries. *William C. Janssen*

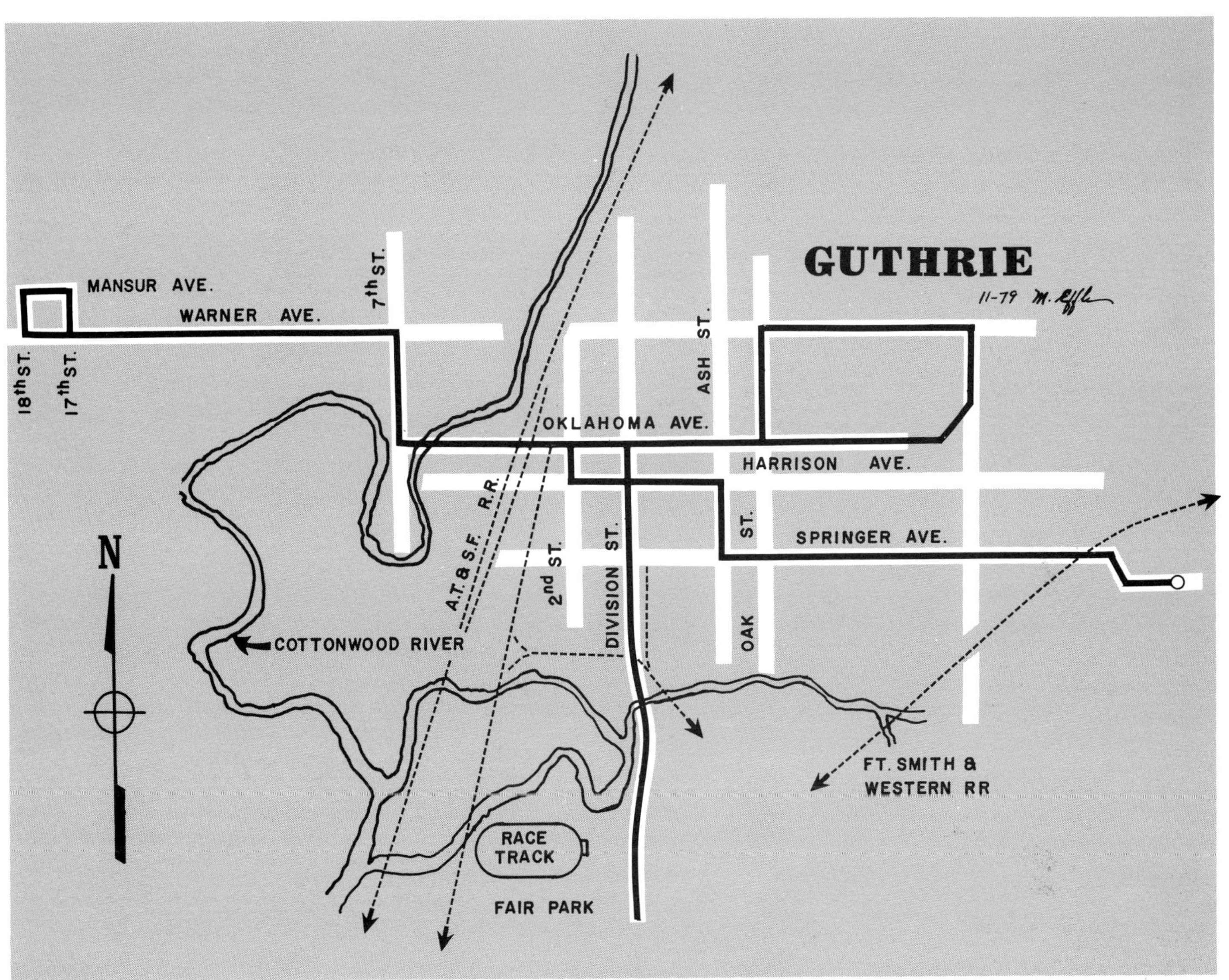

METROPOLITAN RY. CO. (Chartered 1-28-1902, opened 2-8-1903) OKLAHOMA CITY RY. CO. Inc. (6-15-1904, acq. Metro 7-1-1904)
Name changed to OKLAHOMA RAILWAY CO. 1907

Original Roster:

FLEET NO.		BUILDER	ORDER	DATE	REMARKS
M	1-8	American	450	1903	ST closed city. New.
OC	9-16	American	450E	1904	ST closed city. New. Detroit rear platform.
ORy	17-22	American	805	1909	ST closed city. New.
ORy	23-24	Niles	?	1910	DT interurban. Ex-El Reno Int Ry 1-2; Re# 214-215
ORy	25	St Louis	269	2-11-02	DT interurban. Ex-Cinc Georgetown & Ptsmth, Re# 211
ORy	26	St Louis	469	6-6-04	DT closed city. New. Re# 66
ORy	27-28	St Louis	269	2-11-02	DT interurban. Ex-CG&P. Re# 212-213
ORy	29	Niles	?	1910	DT interurban. Ex-El Reno Int Ry 3. Re# 216.
ORy	30-35	American	850	1910	ST closed city. New.
ORy	36-39	Danville	544	1910	ST closed city. New.
M	41-44	St Louis	?	1903	ST open motor. Acq from St Louis stock. Re# 136-139
M	45 46	St Louis	?	1904	ST 8 bench open trailer. Re# 140-141
M	47-51	St Louis	411	1904	ST 10 bench open trailer. Re# 142-146
M	52-53	St Louis	565?	5-31-05	ST open trailer. Re# 147-148
ORy	54-57	Co shops	?	1907	DT closed convertible. New.
ORy	58-61	American	806	1909	DT closed city. New.
ORy	62-64	Co shops	?	1915	DT freight trailer. Re# 431-432.
ORy	65-72	Pullman	?	?	DT closed trailers. Re# 152-159.

NOTE: Above trailers acquired c.1918 from Southern Public Utilities Co., Charlotte, NC (200-207?); originally
New York elevated trailers. Acquired for use to Camp Greene. Motorized at unk date.

ORy	73-74	?	?	?	DT closed trailers. Re# 160-161. Acq. 2nd hand; reblt 1915.
OC	101-104	St Louis	699	1-10-06	DT closed city. New. Re# 62-65.
ORy	111-114	Co shops	?	1907	DT closed city. New. Re# 50-53.
ORy	121-130	Niles	?	1910	DT closed city. New. All reblt and Re# (124,125,127 to 201-203).
ORy	131-136	Co shops	?	1908	DT closed city. New. Re# 44-49.

THE GUTHRIE RAILWAY CO. (Controlled by Oklahoma Ry.)

1-5	American	579	5-3-05	ST closed city. New.

In 1918, had 9 cars, 6.5 miles of track.

OKLAHOMA RAILWAY CO. Roster after renumberings and later additions:

Numbers	Builder	Lot	Date	Description
1-8	American	450	1903	ST closed city. New.
9-16	American	450E	1904	ST closed city. New. Detroit rear platform.
17-22	American	805	1909	ST closed city. New.
30-35	American	850	1910	ST closed city. New.
36-39	Danville	544	1910	ST closed city. New.
44-49	Co shops		1906	DT closed city. Ex 131-136.
50-53	Co shops		1907	DT closed city. Ex 111-114.
54-57	Co shops		1907	DT convertible city.
58-61	American	806	1909	DT closed city. New.
62-65	St Louis	699	1-10-06	DT closed city. Ex 101-104.
66	St Louis	469	6-6-04	DT closed city. Ex 26.
69-74	St Louis	1139	1-23-17	DT closed city.
75-80	St Louis	1105	1917	DT closed city.
81-88	St Louis	1054	1915	DT closed city.
89-94	St Louis	1080	1915	DT closed city. 91 conv. to utility car; 94 wrecked.
94-96	Jewett	?	1908	DT closed city. Acq. 1918 Denver & Intrbn (Ft.Collins) M105-M107.
101-110	American	1096	1918	ST closed¹ city. New.
111-120	St Louis	1508	2-23-29	DT lwt city. Sold 1947 Mexico City 170-179.
121-130	St Louis	1535	4-2-30	DT lwt city. Sold 1947 Mexico City 180-189.
131-140	St Louis	1536	4-2-30	DT lwt city.
141-150	Kuhlman		1927	DT lwt city. Acq. 1936 Detroit United/East. Mich 3250-3259.
151-153	American	1445	1927	DT lwt interurban. Acq. 1936 Rockford Public Svc (Ill).
121-130	Niles	?	1910	DT closed city. All reblt. 124,125,127 Re# to 201-203.
136-139	St Louis	?	1903	ST open motor. Ex 41-44.
140-141	St Louis	?	1904	ST open trailer. Ex 45-46.
142-146	St Louis	411	1904	ST open trailer. Ex 47-51.
147-148	St Louis	565?	5-31-05	ST open trailer. Ex 52-53.
152-159	Pullman	?	?	DT closed motor. Ex 65-72. See original list for origins.
160-161	?	?	?	DT closed trailer. Ex 73-74. Second hand.
200	Niles	?	1910	DT interurban motor. Reblt from 122-130 class in 1912.
201-203	Niles	?	1910	DT interurban motor. Reblt from 124,125,127 in 1915.
211	St Louis	269	2-11-02	DT interurban motor. Ex 25; orig. Cin Georgetown & Ptsmth.
212-213	St Louis	269	2-11-02	DT interurban motor. Ex 27-28; Orig. CG&P.
214-216	Niles	?	1910	DT interurban motor. Ex 23,24,29; Orig. El Reno Int. 1-3.
217-220	St Louis	1106	6-1-16	DT interurban motor. New.
221-224	St Louis	1314A	5-22-23	DT interurban lwt motor. Acq. 1932 Ft.Wayne-Lima RR.
225-229	American	1445	1927	DT interurban lwt motor. Acq. 1936 Rockford Pub. Svc. 300-306.
232-234	St Louis	1361	2-5-25	DT interurban lwt motor. Acq. 1943 Springfield & Xenia (Ohio) 162-164.
235-239	Cincinnati	2140	1916	DT interurban motor. Acq. 1944 Schenectady Ry. (NY) 650-654.
300-319	Cincinnati	2480	1923	ST Birneys. New.
320-322	American	1304	5/1922	ST Birneys. Acq. San Diego Elec. Ry. (Calif.) 332-334.
400	Co shops	?	1913	DT freight motor. Reblt to line car.
401-402	Niles	?	1910	DT freight motor. Reblt from pass. car in 121-130 series, 1913.
403-404	Niles	?	1910	DT freight motor. Reblt from pass. car in 121-130 series, 1916.

NOTE: Above four cars reconverted to passenger use in 1943.

431-433	Co shops	?	1914	DT freight trailer. Ex 62-64.
500	Co shops	?	1913	DT interurban line car.
501	Co shops	?	1911	ST city line car.
600	Co shops	?	1910	Elec.. locomotive; reblt 1929. Sold 1946 to Mason City & Clr Lake 50; to Iowa Terminal 50. Scrapped 4-1063.
601	Co shops	?	1907	Elec. locomotive; reblt 1929. Scrapped 1947.
602	Co shops	?	1918	Elec. locomotive. Scrapped 1947.
603-604	Co shops	?	1929	Elec. locomotives. Both sold 1946 to Union Elec. (Kan.) 603-604; Sold 1954 Chic Aurora & Elgin 4004-4005. Scrapped 1963.
605	Co shops	?	1929	Elec. locomotive. Sold 1946? Amer Aggregates Corp. 605, Re#5095. Used at Green Oaks, Mich., as diesel loco.
606	Co shops	?	1929	Elec. locomotive. Sold 1946? Niagara Jct. Ry. (NY) 12. Scrapped 1952.

2. A TOONERVILLE TRAGEDY

FOR A CITY its size—less than 5,000 citizens—Clinton, Oklahoma, was well endowed with mainline railroads in 1909. No less than three intersected in the largest city in Custer County and strategic way-point between Oklahoma City and Amarillo. They were the Kansas City, Mexico & Orient, the Frisco and the Rock Island.

But the fact that the lines crossed north of the main business district dictated that two passenger stations had to be located more than a mile apart, and in 1909 a group of Clinton businessmen decided to organize a company to build a streetcar line between the old Orient depot west of downtown and the Frisco/Rock Island station east of the business district.

What resulted was one of the shortest, unluckiest and most short-lived streetcar lines in Oklahoma, if not the entire midwest.

The Clinton Street Railway Co. laid down a single track on Frisco Ave. between the two depots and opened service in June of 1909. The system was simplicity itself—one track, one car—a Fairbanks-Morse Type 19 which was propelled by a gasoline engine. The promoters, who included R.O. Hunt, C.G. Welch, Herman Smith, Harry I. Quiett, Charles Goodwin, Dell West and Bill Crawford, could not afford to electrify the line.

Breakdowns were frequent, and nobody knew how to repair the 19-passenger, four-wheeled car which bore CSR fleet number 1. By 1911 service had ceased and train passengers were again hoofing it between depots. The track remained and in 1912 the company was sold to a group headed by W.R. Thompson, vice president and manager.

Somewhat surprisingly, Thompson and his backers raised more than $7,000 to erect trolley wire and put up a small substation. Crawford was president of the reorganized company and Smith became secretary-treasurer. In mid-1912, a second-hand, double-truck trolley car arrived from Chicago, where it had been bought on the installment plan, and passenger service in Clinton resumed.

Dell West was the motorman of the single car, and his daily passengers became accustomed to his cry of "Thom-m-mpsonvill-l-e" whenever the trolley would pass the intersection of Frisco Avenue and Eighth Street, where lived manager Thompson.

For an all-too-brief period, optimism prevailed on the Clinton Street Railway. Its backers talked earnestly of extending the tracks north to Arapaho, the county seat, and ultimately, perhaps, to Taloga, 40 miles further.

But on August 27, 1914, the electric car, making its shuttle run from the Orient depot eastward to the Frisco station, failed to make a customary stop before crossing a Frisco spur line at the Newkirk elevator near the depot. At that moment a Frisco switch engine was bearing down on the crossing, and the streetcar was struck and demolished. One passenger was killed, and five other passengers injured.

Lawsuits quickly rendered the company insolvent, and service was never resumed. During 1915 Smith salvaged the tracks to help pay the legal bills, but the original investors lost just about everything. Thus ended the short history of public transport in Custer County; Clinton never again had so much as a city bus line.

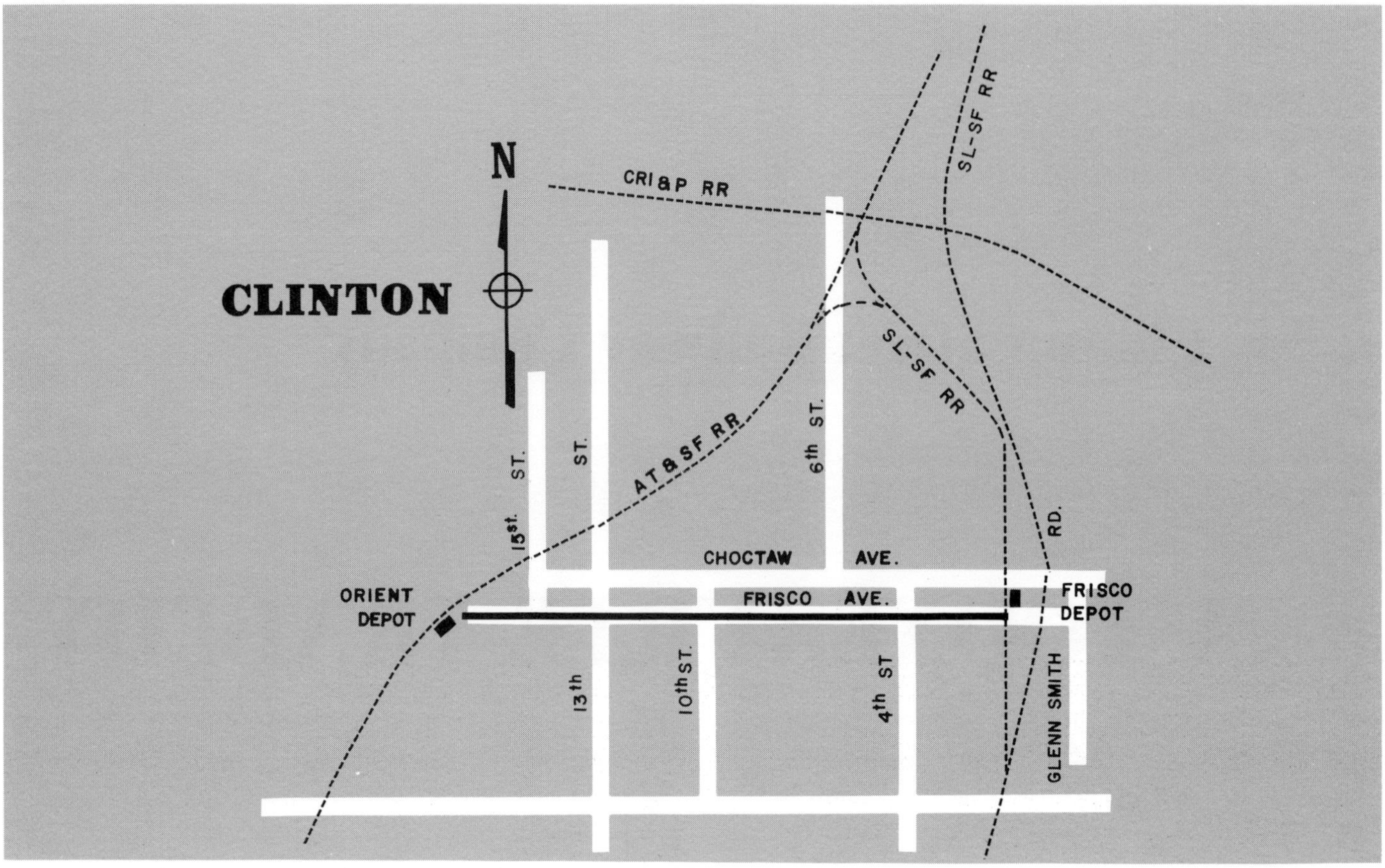

Fairbanks-Morse self-propelled gasoline car provided all service on Clinton's early streetcar line. Side curtains rolled down to protect against Western Oklahoma thunderstorms.
Preston George Collection

3. TROOPS *and* TROLLEYS

IN THE YEARS immediately prior to statehood, the sparsely populated Southwest sector of Oklahoma gave little promise of spawning what was to become the state's third most populous metropolitan area. It was Indian country with a growing agricultural base. And it had Fort Sill, a U.S. Army cavalry post which dated back to Civil War days.

About six miles south of Fort Sill was the town of Lawton. As agriculture and commerce moved into the area after the turn of the century, Lawton started growing into the region's commercial center.

Inevitably, it was not long before agitation began for some kind of public transportation—a streetcar line based on the new electric railway technology. Several groups of investors came to town, announced plans for construction of a line, and promptly disappeared. For several years, frustration and false starts were Lawton's lot.

About 1908 or 1909 unidentified individuals were granted a franchise for a line to be known either as the Lawton Northwestern Electric Co. or the Lawton & Fort Sill Railway Co., the records not disclosing which name was official. Some construction actually was carried out, to the extent of laying track from about 3rd Street to the vicinity of North Boundary (now Gore Blvd.)

Then, all work ceased and the project lay dormant. In 1912 the Lawton & Fort Sill Railway Co., by then defunct, was sold to M.A. Wert of the Bank of Lawton. On February 15 of that year B.R. Stephens and L.E. Fisher, representing the McKinley interests (owners of the Illinois Traction System and some lines in Kansas) arrived in Lawton to look the situation over.

They were met at the depot by State Senator (later U.S. Sen.) Elmer Thomas, N.A. Robertson, Charles N. Holt, and other local businessmen and were escorted around Lawton, Fort Sill and Medicine Park, a largely undeveloped recreation area in the mountains northwest of Fort Sill.

Negotiations began for a right-of-way through the military reservation, and discussions initiated about a franchise in the city of Lawton. This kicked up a brief but furious civic controversy over the prospective company's demand for $15,000 worth of prepaid transportation and bonuses and a five-year waiver of taxes—plus a 25-year franchise.

Despite some further construction, mostly involving the uncovering of the tracks laid previously by the defunct company, the negotiations became bogged down in controversy and finally ground to a halt. The Illinois traction men returned home, and Lawton remained a city without streetcars.

But the town continued to grow, and two years later the

streetcar project was again revived, this time by B.R. Stephens, part owner of the Choctaw Electric and Lighting Co. of McAlester, on the east side of Oklahoma. Work on the line resumed, this time in earnest.

All during the Spring of 1914, Lawton's local newspapers, the *Constitution* and the *Daily News and Star,* were full of hopeful harbingers of streetcars to come. On May 2, 1914, the *News and Star* reported that:

> While no street cars are as yet ringing the bell down C Avenue, the prospects of that very condition in the very near future are exceedingly bright. Friday Construction Engineer Yarbrough received the bill of lading for the steel rails and the cars will arrive within a few days. Five car loads of ties arrived in the yards Friday and the bill of lading has been received for the five remaining cars. The additional boiler for the power plant has been shipped and its bill of lading, as well as one for a car of coal, is now in the hands of Mr. Yarbrough. The remaining poles will arrive early in the week as will the greater portion of overhead . . .

orders for the cars have already been placed and it sure appears that the welcome clang of the street car gong is not going to be long postponed.

Finally, on Saturday, July 11, 1914, two summer-type open streetcars began regular schedules between Lawton and Fort Sill. The first ceremonial run carried a group of Army dignitaries and city officials from the army post into town. The *News and Star* exulted:

> Listen for the gong of the first street car that traverses a Lawton business street. A dream of eight years will be realized Saturday! There have been blasted hopes, several financial miscalculations, a number of newspaper interurbans built, but at last the real thing is here and, unless plans miscarry, cars will start operating on schedule Saturday morning.

The newspaper reported that cars would leave the city hourly for Fort Sill, with a 40-minute service planned for later; perhaps "even a thirty minute service on busy days."

The company, formally known as the Lawton Railway &

Interurban car has just arrived in downtown Lawton from Fort Sill, and khaki-clad soldiers scramble off. The year was 1917, and the army post was busy gearing up for America's entry into World War I.
Floyd Tice Collection, Museum of the Great Plains

Light Co., struggled along briefly with just the two cars, but shortly afterward added two trailers, wooden single-truckers 34 feet long.

Although tracks had been laid from Seventh and C Streets in downtown Lawton, regular service began at the intersection of Third Street, continued east to Second, and turned north toward the fort, passing the carbarn and powerhouse at what is now Ferris Ave. The single track then paralleled the Frisco and Rock Island railroads to the post. An additional track was laid from Second and C streets east two blocks to the Rock Island depot but saw little, if any, regular service.

Highway 277 was later built partly on the interurban's right-of-way. At the railway station at Fort Sill, the electric line's tracks veered northwest, paralleling the road where Snow Hall now stands, turned west on the south side of the old guardhouse and the cemetery, turned north on Fort Sill Blvd. to a final stop opposite the old Officers Quarters.

Important stops on the line were at the Comanche Reformed Missions, Rogers Lane, Post Field Gate, the Rock Island depot at Fort Sill, and the Indian School.

It cost some $127,000 to build the 6.31-mile line, with $50,000 being spent on cars and equipment. The line boasted 11 bridges. The track was constructed of 60-pound rails with most of the overhead built of bracket suspension from 30-foot 6-inch poles utilizing 3.0 round wire. Many of the crossties were of black walnut from Arkansas.

The line's two cars groaned under the initial flood of traffic, but two more cars were delivered by the end of summer; these, fortunately, were closed cars more suitable for Oklahoma winters.

Nineteen fourteen was the year war broke out in Europe, and within two years Fort Sill was put on a wartime footing. By 1916 Lawton's population was 7,788 and eight cars were on the property, one of which was retired in 1918. Fort Sill's wartime population reached 60,000 soldiers, and a 30-minute interurban schedule was barely adequate to handle the khaki-clad crowds. Cars ran continuously from 6:00 A.M. to midnight, every day.

During its first seven years, the streetcars carried some six million fares—two million of them during 1918 alone, the peak year. One of the original motormen was Floyd Tice

It was a hot day out at Fort Sill in the summer of 1917, and this Lawton-bound open trolley is already crawling with doughboys eager for an outing in town. The motorman is Floyd Tice who, in 1978, was still around to provide photos and background on the line. The conductor was Fred Gragg.
Fred Gragg Collection, Museum of the Great Plains

who, more than a half-century later at age 85, was still providing clear descriptions of the operation. The years 1917 and 1918 were extremely busy, and the car crews worked long hours to transport the troops.

"We had to have military policemen ride the cars to keep the soldier boys off the roof," he recalled. An occasional passenger in those days, and Tice remembers the bespectacled officer quite well, was Capt. Harry S Truman who was stationed at Camp Doniphan, an outpost beyond the end of the car line.

The interurbans were the only link between the army post and the various recreations of Lawton, and weekends especially taxed the system.

The company's business office was first located at Third and C, later at 426 C Avenue where a combination station and cafe was located. Many years later, the restaurant was still known as the Terminal Cafe. Stephens was president of the company until shortly before the end.

The war was over by 1919, and Fort Sill shrank to a more normal few thousand military men who were beginning to acquire automobiles. In 1921, plans were announced to sell bonds to construct an extension to Medicine Park. The project was to cost $300,000 and would involve nine miles of new track beyond the end of the line at Fort Sill, with a terminal near the Medicine Park Hotel; total distance from Lawton would have been 15 miles.

It was hoped to offer four trips daily in the winter months, and hourly service in the summer, at a round-trip fare of 75 cents. However, the bond issue failed to attract investors, and the crowds went to Medicine Park in automobiles.

For awhile, enough business remained between Lawton and Fort Sill to pay expenses, but around 1925 two motor buses were purchased to help out on the Fort Sill route, and to start a service to Medicine Park. Then the company went into receivership, and all rail service was ended on November, 11, 1927. The city's population was still less than 10,000 (it was to grow to more than 70,000 by 1978) and a permanent city bus service was never successful.

Paving and highway projects eventually obliterated all traces of the streetcar system, and most city residents find it hard to believe the clang of the trolley was ever heard in Lawton.

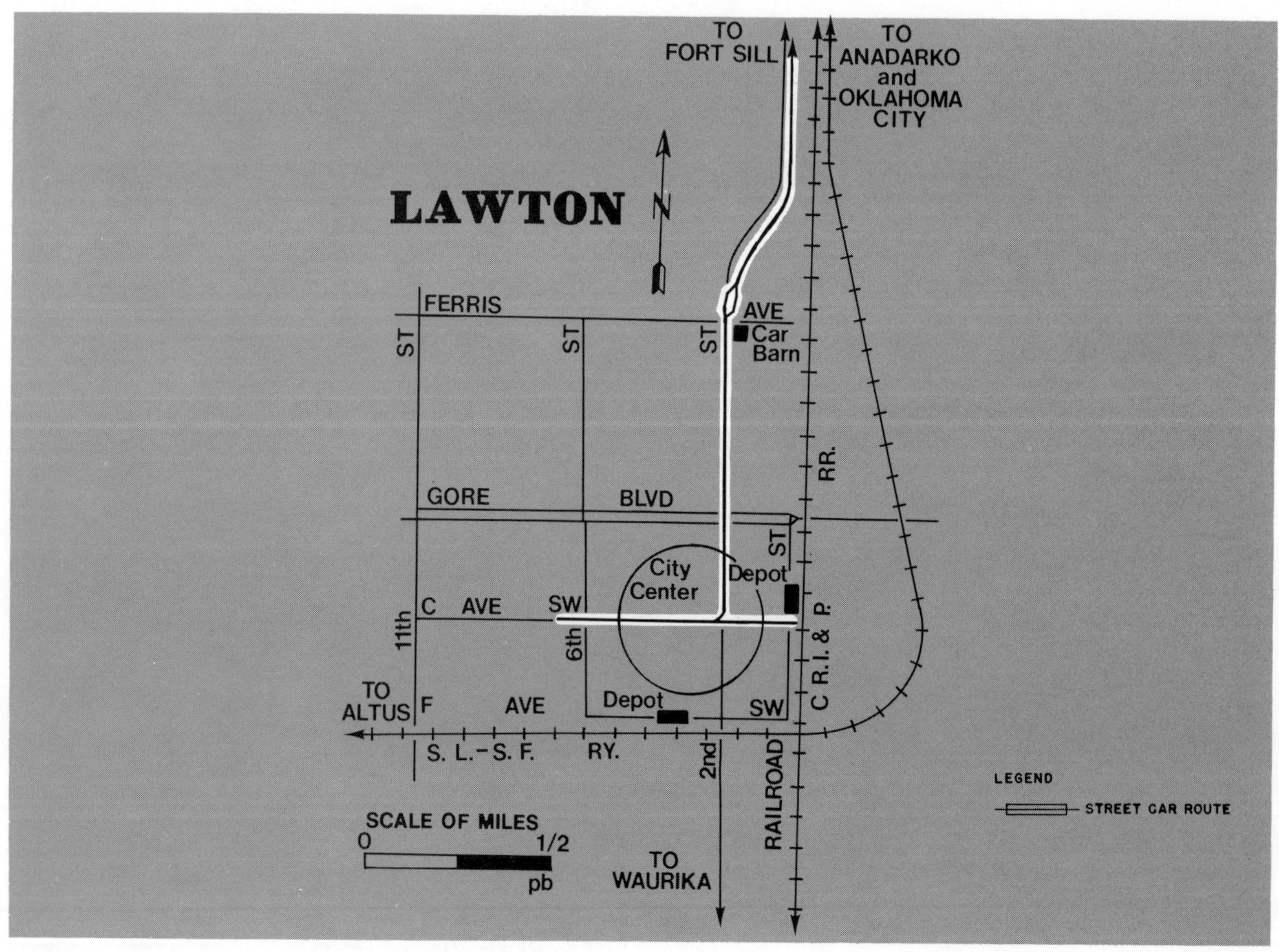

TOP: Moment of quiet on the Fort Sill reservation is observed by motorman Floyd Tice, left, and conductor Fred Gragg, while cameraman snaps their 32-passenger single-truck car. It was midsummer, 1917.

Fred Gragg Collection, Museum of the Great Plains

BOTTOM: Paint is barely dry on the block lettering on the front of open car 1, stopping for a photograph to be taken at Fort Sill, 1917.

Charles V. Hess Photo from Stephen D. Maguire

TOP: Dented dasher of closed car 7 is prominently in evidence at the Fort Sill terminal, as doughboys in breeches and puttees await chance to board for a ride to Lawton, 1917.

Charles V. Hess Photo from Stephen D. Maguire

BOTTOM: With artillery pieces in background, open car of the Lawton Railway & Light Co. bowls along the Fort Sill military reservation in 1919.

Floyd Tice Collection, Museum of the Great Plains

LAWTON RAILWAY & ELECTRIC COMPANY

FLEET NO.	BUILDER	ORDER	DATE	REMARKS
(2 cars)	Brill	19417	6-5-14	DT 12 bench open tlr. New. Orig. blt for F.C.Elec-rico Lerdo a Torreon.
(1 car)	Wason		1910	ST closed city.
(1 car)	Wason		1910	DT closed city.
(2 cars)	Laclede		1895	DT closed city. Acq. 11/15 from Phila. Rapid Transit 706,717; orig. Phila. Transit 1006,1017.

6 miles of track. In 8/1918 had 7 motor passenger cars.

Chickasha Street Railway

4. TAKE ME OUT TO THE BALL GAME

SITUATED about halfway between Oklahoma City and Lawton, Oklahoma's first and third population centers, Chickasha has had a stable population of between 10,000 and 15,000 for nearly seven decades. It was big enough in 1910 to boast a modest streetcar system.

The line was built by local interests and opened on July 12, 1910. On the first day of operation, 1,615 fares were collected; earnings the first year exceeded $20,000, not unusual for a small-town trolley system in the immediate pre-automobile era.

Chickasha's system, called the Chickasha Street Railway, was six and a half miles long and utilized seven single-truck electric cars, some of them the open-air summer type. Three of the cars (one closed and two open) were bought used from the Boston Elevated Railway, having been built in 1889 and 1892; thus they were nearly 20 years old when entering service in Chickasha. The other four cars were purchased new from Brill and arrived a few months after service began.

Repair shops and barn were at 19th Street and Dakota Avenue. The system as constructed began at the Rock Island Depot downtown and ran via Chickasha Ave. and 9th Street to Dakota. From that point the line looped via Dakota, 19th, Alabama Ave. and 9th St., reaching the home of what later became the Oklahoma College for Women, now the Oklahoma College of Liberal Arts. A spur line, built later, continued south on 19th Street to Montana, turning east to 13th and passing the University Park baseball field at Shannon Springs. Eventually this line was connected up with the main line via new track on 13th Street.

As was typical, the line ran into trouble with the coming of the automobile, even though Chickasha's population of 10,320 in 1910 grew to 15,447 by 1916. By 1923 six trolleys were in revenue service along with one non-revenue car; the ball park extension, however, was amputated. Fares were 7 cents, or 15 tickets for $1.00; children were entitled to buy 30 tickets for a dollar.

Special events were a terrific traffic generator for the early-day trolley lines, and one of the biggest days the Chickasha Street Railway ever had occurred on October 25,

1914, when the famed baseball idol Walter P. Johnson pitched at the University Park diamond at Shannon Springs.

The neighboring town teams of Minco and Geary staged an exhibition game, well after the end of regular big league season play, with "Big Train" pitching for Minco. Johnson fanned 11 batters, allowed two hits and Minco won, 6-0. Alas, despite 1,050 paid admissions (mostly carried by the streetcars), the game's promoters lost $450.

By the mid-1920s, there were few persons living in towns the size of Chickasha still dependent on public transportation, and on August 7, 1927, the company threatened to shut down. Pleas from the city fathers induced the company to struggle along for another week, but service was then suspended.

Apparently no serious attempt was made to revive the operation, for the power lines were dismantled after a short legal squabble was settled, and some of the cars reportedly were sold for further use in South America.

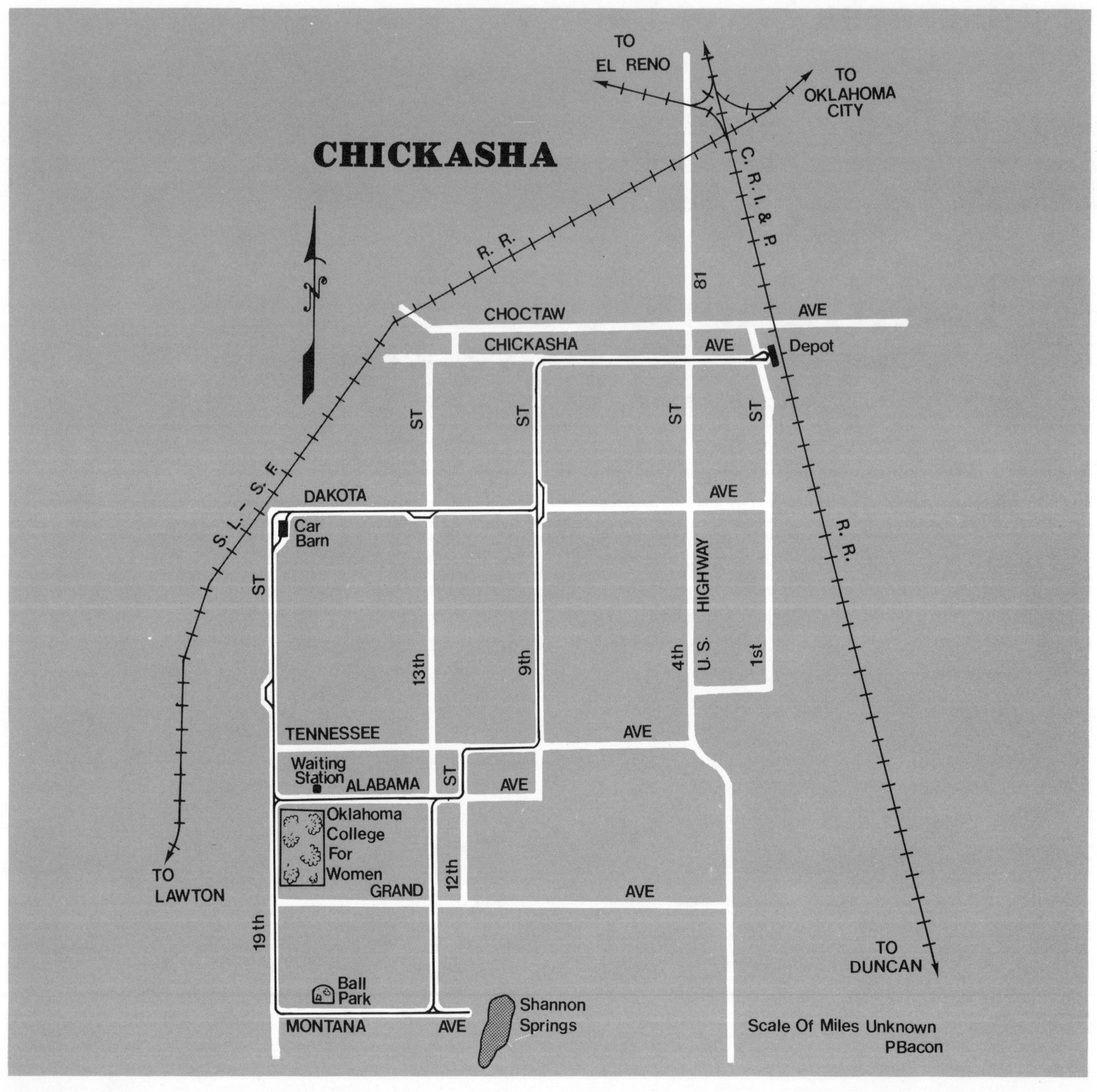

Proud crew poses beside Chickasha Street Railway car 5 in this early view. Unfortunately, glass plate negative cracked, nearly slicing off the northeast corner of the car. *Irvin W. Munn Collection*

This is the way they used to pack 'em aboard Chickasha's trolleys—especially on a red letter day like October 25, 1914, when Walter "Big Train" Johnson pitched a baseball game for the Minco nine. Johnson fanned 11 batters, allowed two hits and Minco blanked Geary, 6-0. The next year Johnson won his 200th major league baseball game. Even though the promoters of the exhibition game lost $450, the cars of the Chickasha Street Railway chalked up a nice profit. Lead trolley in this procession carries a "Dakota Avenue" sign. *Irvin W. Munn Collection*

Chickasha Ave. and Third Street looked like this in 1911. Streetcar is about to pick up a quartet of paying passengers.
Irvin W. Munn Collection

CHICKASHA STREET RAILWAY

FLEET NO.	BUILDER	ORDER	DATE	REMARKS
(1 car)	Jones		1892	ST closed city. Ex-Boston Elevated Ry. 1218.
(2 cars)	Jones		1889	ST 7 bench open. Ex-Boston Elev. 2046,2049; orig. West End Elec.
				Rebuilt from horsecars in Boston
4	Brill	17490	9-29-10	ST semiconvertible. New.

6.5 miles of track. In 8/1918 had 7 motor cars.

Ardmore Traction Company

5. LITTLE SYSTEM IN LITTLE DIXIE

LIKE MOST small cities experiencing rapid growth in the early years of the twentieth century, Ardmore, at the foot of the Arbuckle Mountains in south-central Oklahoma, wanted a streetcar line. Before the automotive age, public transportation was an absolute necessity for city growth, the opening of new housing subdivisions and public attractions beyond the center of town.

To meet this need, the Ardmore Traction Co. was organized in the Fall of 1905, with construction beginning immediately and service opening in January 1906. The company was capitalized at $500,000; five cars were obtained new from the American Car Co. in St. Louis to open service. There may have been a couple of second-hand cars from Fort Worth, Texas, on hand as well.

Ardmore's population reached 16,000 within a year, making it the capital of that part of Oklahoma sometimes known as "Little Dixie"; and by January 1908 the company was constructing an extension north three miles to Lorena Park. Four more cars arrived from the St. Louis Car Co.

The streetcar line ran west from the Santa Fe Depot through Ardmore's business section, thence northwest to Hargrove College. The Lorena Park terminus boasted such attractions as a baseball diamond, picnic areas, a fishing lake, a swimming pool and playgrounds. Nearby was the Dornick Hills Country Club, another source of trolley car patronage.

Locating such attractions at the outer end of the line was done deliberately to stimulate traffic, and Ardmore's trolley fleet included a number of "convertible" cars whose solid sides could be removed and replaced by screens for a breezy summer ride. Standard streetcar fare was a nickel, or a dime all the way to the park.

By 1909 the roster contained a total of 10 cars, but within a short time some of the cars were sold and by 1918 only four cars were listed. Business failed to live up to expectations from the first; the company was in receivership as early as 1910 and the name changed to the Ardmore Electric Railway Co. By this time trackage totaled 3.37 miles.

The company did not generate its own power, but purchased it from Consumers Light & Power Co. Ardmore's streetcars limped along through World War I, but by 1920 the company was losing $100 to $400 per month, and received permission to raise fares to a straight 10 cents. The timing could not have been worse, for it coincided with a recession and the public's new-found mania for the Model T.

In 1922 the company petitioned for total abandonment. Permission was quickly granted, and Ardmore's streetcars quickly became a memory.

Builders photos show Ardmore Traction cars 15 and 18. The company purchased both single- and double-truck cars; running board on car 18 reveals that it can be converted to an "open" car in the summertime.

Railway Negative Exchange; Sprague Library

This was downtown Ardmore in horse-and-buggy days. Streetcars were a paying business so long as the streets were devoid of automobiles, as in this scene.

Mac McGailliard Collection

One of Ardmore's double-truck convertible cars, possibly Number 18, sits just outside the Ardmore Traction Co. car-barn in this 1917 view. Snow on the ground was a bit unusual in Little Dixie, but by no means unknown.
Mac McGailliard Collection from Earl Holloway

ARDMORE TRACTION COMPANY

FLEET NO.	BUILDER	ORDER	DATE	REMARKS
(5 cars)	American	565	5-22-05	DT closed city. New. 1 sold 1908 to Okla Interurban Ry.
1-4	StLouis	786	2-20-08	ST closed city. New.
15	American	797A	1909	ST closed city. New.
(1 car)	American	797B	1909	ST closed city. New.

CERA Bulletin 80 says 2 open cars and 4 DT interurban cars acquired in 1908. In 8/1918 had 4 motor cars, 1 other, 3.37 miles of track.

Enid City Railway

6. WHERE STREETCARS WERE ILLEGAL

ONE DAY in August 1889 the Rock Island Railroad, building south from Kansas into Oklahoma, reached a point about 100 miles northwest of Oklahoma City. The great green prairie lay in the Cherokee Strip, which was not to be opened for another four years, and no white man could remain there without a special permit.

M.A. Low, president of the Rock Island, put down the *Idylls of the King* he had been reading and with a group of officials alighted from the private train.

"What," he inquired, "is the name of this place?" The town boasted only a few shacks.

"Skeleton," was the answer. "The Skeleton Stage Line used to run through here."

Low shook his head. "That won't do at all. Let's see . . ." pausing, Low's thoughts reverted to the Knights of the Round Table in the book he had just been reading, to Geraint, and his beautiful wife, Enid.

"Enid will be the name of this town," he said.

The opening of the Cherokee Strip in 1893 brought an influx of settlers, and between 1897 and 1903 the Santa Fe and Frisco railroads built into Enid; by 1900 Enid had become a grain and trade center of some 3,500; by 1910, 13,799.

The town was spreading out and on January 4, 1907, the Enid City Railway was incorporated and given a 50-year franchise to operate streetcars. The owners included promoter C.H. Bosler of Dayton, Ohio, and they capitalized the new company at $235,000. Bosler was also instrumental in building the Tulsa Street Railway.

Revenue service began June 3 of that year; early car purchases included two open and four closed single-truck cars from the American Car Co., St. Louis. By the end of the first year, the company had grossed $20,164.

Throughout the company's 22-year existence, two routes were operated on a system resembling a large cross, with all cars meeting at the courthouse. One line ran east and west on Broadway, jogging on the east side via 12th and East Maine to serve Phillips University. The other line ran north and south along Grand Ave., with extensions along West Wabash on the southern end and along Independence and Washington on the north side of town.

The basic system totaled six miles of track. From 1907 to about 1910 an extension ran from Phillips University to a livestock pavilion about a mile east of the college. The carbarns were located on West Oklahoma at the Santa Fe tracks, and from about 1907 to 1912 or 1914 an extension was operated from here to Lakewood Park, an amusement park owned by the streetcar company.

Grand Ave. was the weaker of the two lines, although the

TOP: County courthouse dominates this early-day Enid street scene, looking west on East Broadway. Photo may have been taken shortly after inauguration of streetcar service in June of 1907.   *Museum of the Cherokee Strip*

BOTTOM: View from the courthouse steps looking west along Broadway, circa 1907. Single-truck car is taking the curve into Broadway.   *Bill Edson, Enid News & Eagle*

circus grounds were located at the north end, and a plan—never carried out—would have extended the tracks to the city's principal cemetery. This line did serve the Santa Fe and Frisco depots, and ran near the Rock Island depot as well.

Failure of the Lakewood Park extension was especially painful for promoters of the Enid City Railway, who had purchased 76 acres of property alongside it with hopes of subdividing. But the area remained open country for decades after the demise of the electric cars.

The ECRy. reached its peak rather quickly; in 1913 it owned 14 motor cars and six trailers; by 1918 this had dwindled to 10 motor cars and six trailers which were seldom if ever needed. Schedules of the day indicated a 14-minute citywide headway which could be handled by six cars without difficulty.

Enid was a fairly prosperous small city, and the city fathers laid out wide streets with good paving. Consequently the automobile came early and in great numbers, and by the early 1920s the ECRy. was in deep financial trouble. Pleading poverty, the railway refused to pave between the rails on many major streets even after the city had paved the remainder of the thoroughfare.

In 1923 the city and the traction company reached a compromise which permitted the ECRy. to use chat between the rails. This did not stop the complaints from motorists, and friction with the city council increased. The city successfully resisted attempts to increase fares above 7 cents (even after Muskogee, Oklahoma City and Tulsa went to 8 cents) and deferred maintenance of the cars and equipment became a constantly boiling issue.

Further, city officials had to deal with the company's local manager, Morris McGrath, instead of the owners in far-off Dayton and this did not help matters. The absentee owners complained that they had spent some $300,000 on the system which had, over a 20-year period, yielded less than an average one percent return. By 1929, both the city and the company were in a sour mood and headed for a confrontation.

This came the last week of August 1929, after the company had rejected several ultimatums from the city to fix the system's sagging overhead wires and repair faulty tracks. Ignoring the company's 50-year franchise which still had 28 years to run, the city council met on August 29 and passed an ordinance *outlawing* the entire streetcar system.

The ordinance stated that as of the next day ECRy. was

Proud of its newly paved street, unknown photographer captured this civic betterment, along with three trolleys. Photo was taken on February 28, 1908, and looks west on Broadway from the courthouse.

Museum of the Cherokee Strip

not to attempt operating any streetcars, and that "any person or persons found guilty of operating a streetcar . . . will be arrested and fined in police court not to exceed $20."

Nevertheless, the streetcars operated as usual on Friday, August 30, a defiant McGrath vowing that he would continue to send the cars out until physically stopped by the police. Meanwhile, one hapless motorman was actually arrested for the criminal act of operating a streetcar. The trial of A.T. Snowder was set for late September.

Finally, at 9:30 A.M., Saturday, August 31, Chief of Police Calvert showed up at the carbarn and ordered McGrath to call the cars in.

"Will we be arrested if we do not?" asked McGrath.

"You certainly will," replied the Chief.

McGrath pretended continued uncertainty, asking about the quality of the food at the city jail. The Chief said he didn't know, that he had never eaten there, but warned that Mayor Jesse T. Butts was demanding a showdown and that

he, Calvert, would have to act. So McGrath ordered the cars back to the barn and by 11 A.M. Enid's streetcars were off the streets forever.

Meanwhile the city had hurriedly granted a franchise to two Stillwater, Okla., men to operate a replacement bus service, and by noon they had managed to put two borrowed buses on the old car routes.

The city's squabble with the streetcar company was not quite over, however. For the next two weeks the city and ECRy. argued noisily over which would pay for removing the rails and overhead wires. Finally the city lost all patience and did the job itself. On Saturday, September 15, city trucks drew up to the courthouse and crews began cutting overhead wires.

Not surprisingly, seconds after the wires were cut away from the first corner pole, it toppled to the street, graphic testimony to the dilapidated condition of Enid's unlucky streetcar system.

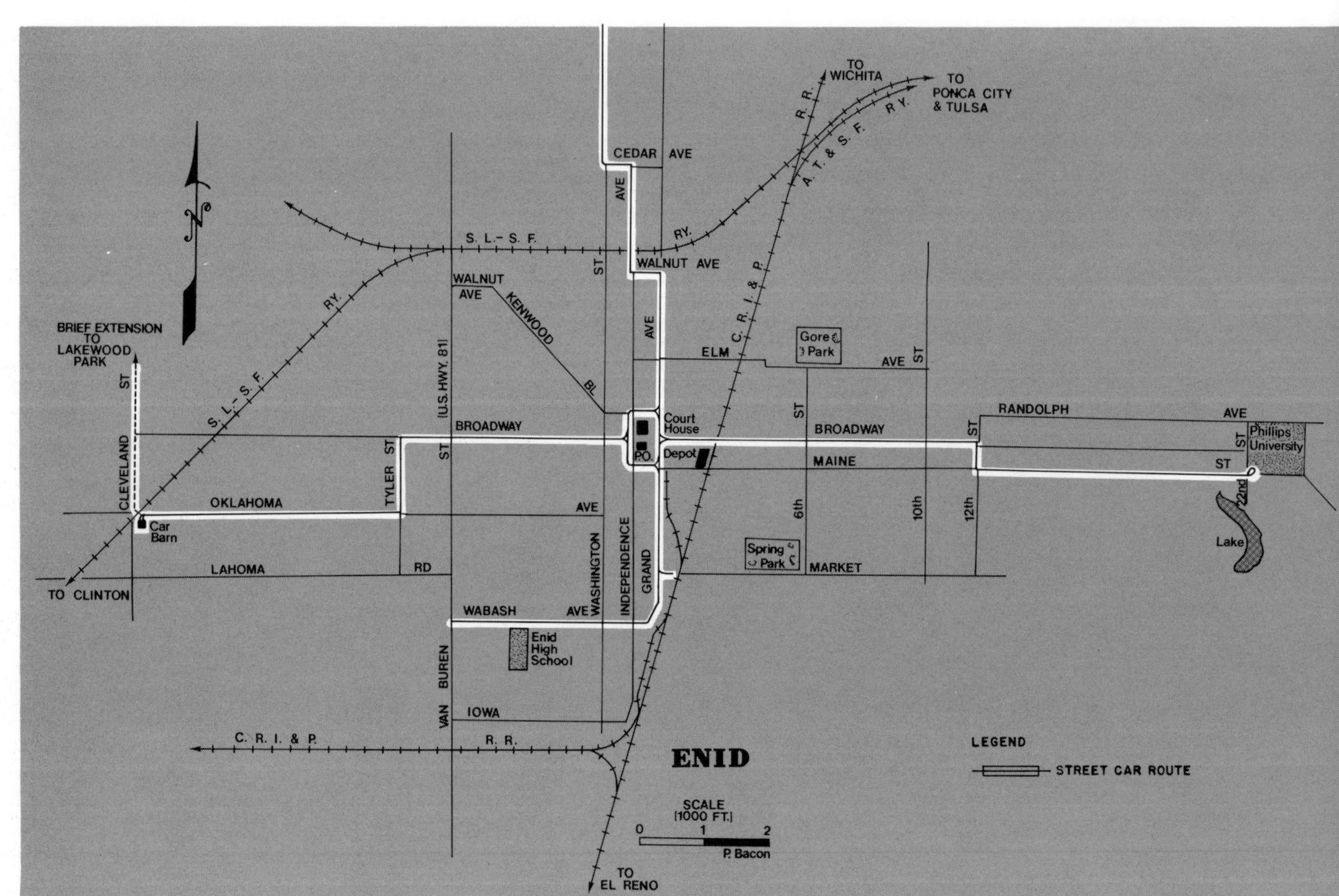

TOP: Nearly every Enid resident was on hand for the circus parade, it seemed, for the annual visit of the Ringling Bros. circus was an eagerly awaited event. Amid all the excitement and confusion is this Enid City Railway single-trucker, seemingly swept along by the procession, corner of Randolph and North Grand. *Bill Edson, Enid News & Eagle*

MIDDLE: July Fourth brought out flags and bunting, and of course another parade. This 1912 photo includes Enid City Railway car 200 in front of the Kennedy Mercantile Co.
George Rainey from Stephen D. Maguire Collection

RIGHT: Open car 100 of Enid City Railway at the corner of Monroe and Broadway, circa 1910. Sprinkler wagon has just moistened street to left of trolley. *Texas ERA Collection*

TOP: Trio of closed cars and the tower car at the Enid City Railway carbarn, sometime in the mid-1920s. The brick structure, located in the 2200 block of West Oklahoma, still stood in 1978; some of the tracks were still visible in the pavement.   *John Lovell Collection*

BOTTOM: After Enid outlawed streetcars, the city pulled up the tracks as soon as possible. Cletrac crawler tractor was used to yank the rails from the pavement. Date was February 26, 1930.

George Rainey from Mrs. Velma Jayne Collection

ENID STREET RAILWAY

FLEET NO.	BUILDER	ORDER	DATE	REMARKS
100,105	American	733	7-15-07	ST 10 bench open. New.
200,205, 210,215	American	737	8-12-07	ST closed city. New.
(1 car)	West End El.		1892	ST closed city. Acq. 1909 Boston Elevated 563; originally horsecar.
(3 cars)	Jones		1889	ST 7 bench open. Acq. 1909 Boston Elevated 2040,2050,2056. "
(1 car)	Barney & Smth		1909?	ST closed city.
(4 cars)	Danville		1910	ST closed city. CERA bulletin 80 says Barney & Smith, builder.
(2 cars)	?		1917	ST closed city. 30' length.

6.92 miles of track. In 8/1918 had 10 motor cars and 6 other cars.

7. TOO MUCH TRANSPORTATION

ONE OF THE smallest links in the chain of companies controlled or managed by the vast Byllesby organization, which included the giant Market Street Railway in San Francisco, was the Shawnee-Tecumseh Traction Co., which operated about 12 miles of line from 1906 to 1927.

An argument over whether Shawnee or Tecumseh should be the county seat of Pottawatomie County had raged for years, with the much-smaller Tecumseh finally winning the question by building a new brick courthouse and jail in 1897.

But Shawnee tried hard to get the seat of government back, and pointed to its much superior transportation facilities. It was on two important railway lines — the Rock Island and the Santa Fe. A third line, the Choctaw, Oklahoma & Gulf, tried to build through Tecumseh, but the city fathers refused to donate land.

Finally, in 1896, Tecumseh's transportation problems were solved when $30,000 was raised and construction started on the Shawnee-Tecumseh Railway Co. In 1900, this branch line, locally nicknamed the "Lillian Russell," carried more than 11,000 bales of cotton out of Tecumseh. In 1903

the short line was bought by the Rock Island, which then extended the branch south to Asher.

Tecumseh's cup runneth over. In that same year, the Santa Fe began extending its line south through Tecumseh and on to Purcell.

But that wasn't all. Tecumseh learned in 1905 that it was to get a third railroad — this one an electric interurban. On August 5 of that year the Shawnee Traction Co. won a 50-year franchise for a streetcar system in Shawnee, and construction began on a three-line system to serve North Broadway, North Kickapoo, East Main and East 11th Street.

On February 16, 1906, the Shawnee-Tecumseh Traction Co. was incorporated to take over the Shawnee city lines and build the six-mile interurban to Tecumseh. The new line was capitalized at $500,000 and was built under the auspices of the Deka Development Co. Revenue passenger service commenced on September 1, 1906. Tecumseh now had three railroads.

The new company started out with 11 electric cars including three interurbans, four closed city cars and four open city cars. With the six-mile interurban, the company owned 12.5 miles of line. Its general offices were in Shawnee and power was purchased from the Shawnee Gas & Electric Co.

Streetcars helped Shawnee to show a healthy population growth, increasing from 3,436 in 1900 to 12,474 in 1910 and an estimated 18,138 in 1916. By 1910, the S-T was carrying one million passengers annually with gross revenues exceeding $55,000 yearly.

When the city of Shawnee donated the land for Oklahoma Baptist University in 1911, it also paid a bonus of $10,000 to the traction company to extend its North Broadway line to the new campus. By the fall of 1914 the line had been completed to within two blocks of OBU, and the university laid a boardwalk of 12-inch planks to the end of the car line. An argument ensued as to whether this constituted service all the way to the campus, so finally in 1917 streetcars reached the campus proper.

As late as 1923 the system operated 9.75 miles of track with 11 cars in service, plus one motor freight car and a service car. The following year, the fare was raised from a nickel to 7 cents. As was happening everywhere, the streetcar company was having trouble making ends meet.

The company abandoned all streetcar and interurban rail service in January 1927, replacing the cars with a fleet of seven buses. Even bus service proved uneconomic, and was suspended in 1931. Finally, in 1934 the Turner Transportation Co. resumed service with a fleet of 15 new buses, and continued the service until at least 1940.

This lineup of Shawnee-Tecumseh streetcars in downtown Shawnee about 1912 probably had something to do with a convention in town. Five trolleys are in this procession, and four of them are open cars. *Oklahoma Historical Society*

TOP: Private right-of-way curved through the woods to reach from Shawnee to Tecumseh. Judging from the well-groomed appearance of the track and the fresh grading, this photo may have been taken shortly after service opened in 1906.

Oklahoma Historical Society

RIGHT: Plethora of railroads in the Shawnee-Tecumseh area is illustrated by this 1906 photo of Shawnee-Tecumseh Traction Co. car out on the right-of-way with two railroad trestles in background.

Stephen D. Maguire Collection

Cancellation on this old postcard dates Shawnee trolley view to early 1906, prior to opening of interurban to Tecumseh. It's a fine view of the "new city hall" and car 4.
Texas ERA Collection

RIGHT: Pair of Shawnee-Tecumseh's larger cars in downtown Shawnee about 1908. Car at right was built by Laclede Car Co., car at left by St. Louis.
E. Harper Charlton from Texas ERA Collection

SHAWNEE-TECUMSEH TRACTION COMPANY

FLEET NO.	BUILDER	ORDER	DATE	REMARKS
(3 cars)	St Louis	631	2-17-06	DT suburban cars. New.
(4 cars)	St Louis	632	2-23-06	DT 12 bench open trailers. New.

In 8/1918 had 10 motor passenger cars and 1 other motor car, 12 mi of track.

8. HOME BREW *and* TROLLEY RIDES

LIKE A NUMBER of Midwestern-Southwestern interurbans such as the Union Electric on the Kansas-Oklahoma border, the Pittsburg County Railway, of McAlester, was short on prospects but long on staying power. The 17-mile line served a tributary population of only about 25,000 persons, but managed to stay in operation from 1903 to 1947, one of the longer spans of any Oklahoma traction system.

The first stirrings of public transportation in this southeastern Oklahoma trading and coal production center occurred in the chartering, on July 26, 1902, of the Indian Territory Traction Co. to build a local streetcar line in McAlester. The 1900 census had given McAlester just 3,479 residents, but the town was growing.

A municipal franchise was granted on December 10, 1902, and construction proceeded on a line linking North McAlester, downtown and the country club area to the southeast. Almost immediately plans developed for an interurban extension to penetrate the strip mine areas immediately to the east of town. A powerhouse and shops were constructed at Busby, northeast of downtown.

Revenue streetcar service began on September 15, 1903, reaching Krebs and Alderson on the new interurban extension at the same time. The interurban was completed and service opened to Hartshorne, its eastern terminus, on November 14, 1904.

In that year the entire enterprise was sold by its local organizers to the Southwest Power Co., originally part of the Alfred Emanuel-National Electric Power syndicate of Dayton, Ohio, but eventually coming under the control of utility magnate Samuel Insull. The combined railway and power company then became known as the Choctaw Railway & Lighting Co.

After Oklahoma's admission to statehood in 1907, growth of the McAlester area intensified. The rugged area just east of McAlester was known for years for two commodities—mining and moonshining—and a locally produced beer which was as delicious as it was illegal. The electric cars were useful for carrying the miners to and from their pits, and perhaps played a small part in transporting the latter as well on certain social occasions, especially to the Saturday night dance.

In 1916 the transfer of control from Emanuel to Insull was completed, and the power system was spun off to become the Choctaw Power and Lighting Co.; the electric railway became the Pittsburg County Railway Co., an affiliate. Six new Birney safety cars of 28-passenger capacity were purchased to modernize the McAlester city route and by 1918 some 16 revenue passenger cars were available for service.

By this time McAlester's population had risen to 18,504. It was the county seat of Pittsburg County, and was the location of the Oklahoma State Prison. More than 26 miles of track were in use with the city fare at 10 cents and interurban fares ranging from 10 cents to 55 cents. Interurban cars generally ran at hourly intervals, with some peak-hour extras.

To economize and make the service more attractive, the railway in 1923 put into service three modern, lightweight interurbans built by the Cincinnati Car Co., replacing a fleet of heavy wooden cars. For some reason, the cars as delivered were set up for two-man operation, an oversight the company was to regret just a few years later. Carload freight business increased, and a second-hand electric freight locomotive was acquired.

The mines at Alderson and Dow continued to provide the PCR with most of its freight revenue, even though the company's trackage was paralleled by the main line of the Rock Island to the south, and a branch of the Katy to the north.

The Depression of the early 1930s brought with it a discontinuance of the McAlester city route and retirement for the six Birney cars, and conversion of the Cincinnati light-

TOP: Rounding the corner at Krebs was green-and-yellow lightweight interurban, November 27, 1941. Note sign on building at left for Progress Beer.
John B. Fink Collection from Charles Winters

RIGHT: One of the lightweight interurbans swings into the McAlester station, 1942. Covered-over tracks in street at left led to the country club before city service was abandoned in the 1930s.
Stephen D. Maguire Collection

weight interurbans to one-man operation. This was not accomplished easily.

The double front doors of the cars were designed for baggage loading from high-level platforms; the cost of rebuilding these doors and adding steps was prohibitive, so instead the decision was made to use existing doors on the left side. From then on passengers had to board the cars from the left, or "wrong" side. Fortunately the line was located on private right-of-way except for the last few blocks in downtown McAlester, so this did not present any great difficulty.

Another timely second-hand acquisition in the late 1930s was a modern steel freight motor, from the Chattanooga Traction Co. in Tennessee. This motor could carry freight and express, and haul 10 fully loaded freight cars as well.

Full corporate independence came about 1940, when the affiliation with Choctaw Power & Lighting was broken. Choctaw became an affiliate of the Public Service Co. of Oklahoma. Guarded optimism over the interurban's future must have prevailed, since the deficits of the 1930s had given way to small profits. Coal operations were stepped up as the nation began to prepare for World War II, and both passenger and freight revenues increased.

But the good times were all too temporary. The end of the war in 1945 brought a sharp drop in freight business, maintenance was cut to the bone, and the line lost $15,000 after taxes in 1946. At the same time, trucks moved in on the strip mine business, so the company sought ICC approval for total abandonment.

The passenger service held up a little better. The 1946 schedule called for 12 daily round trips between McAlester and Hartshorne, with the intermediate town of Haileyville served by a unique "switchback" movement of cars since it was at the end of a short stub track. The full trip took about an hour. There were also some short-turn runs as far as Alderson.

Unexpectedly, the PCR withdrew its petition for total abandonment in November 1946 and asked instead for discontinuance of only the passenger service, hoping somehow to continue freight service. Approval was forthcoming, and the last passenger cars ran on December 2, 1946.

Almost immediately the company realized the hopelessness of its freight operation. New mine closures were announced, and early in 1947 the company applied to the ICC to shut down completely. With the necessary approval in hand quickly, the Pittsburg County Railway abandoned all operations on April 27, 1947. The line was soon scrapped, the cars sold to a salvage company, leaving only the concrete scars on McAlester's downtown streets as reminders of the days of electric interurban cars.

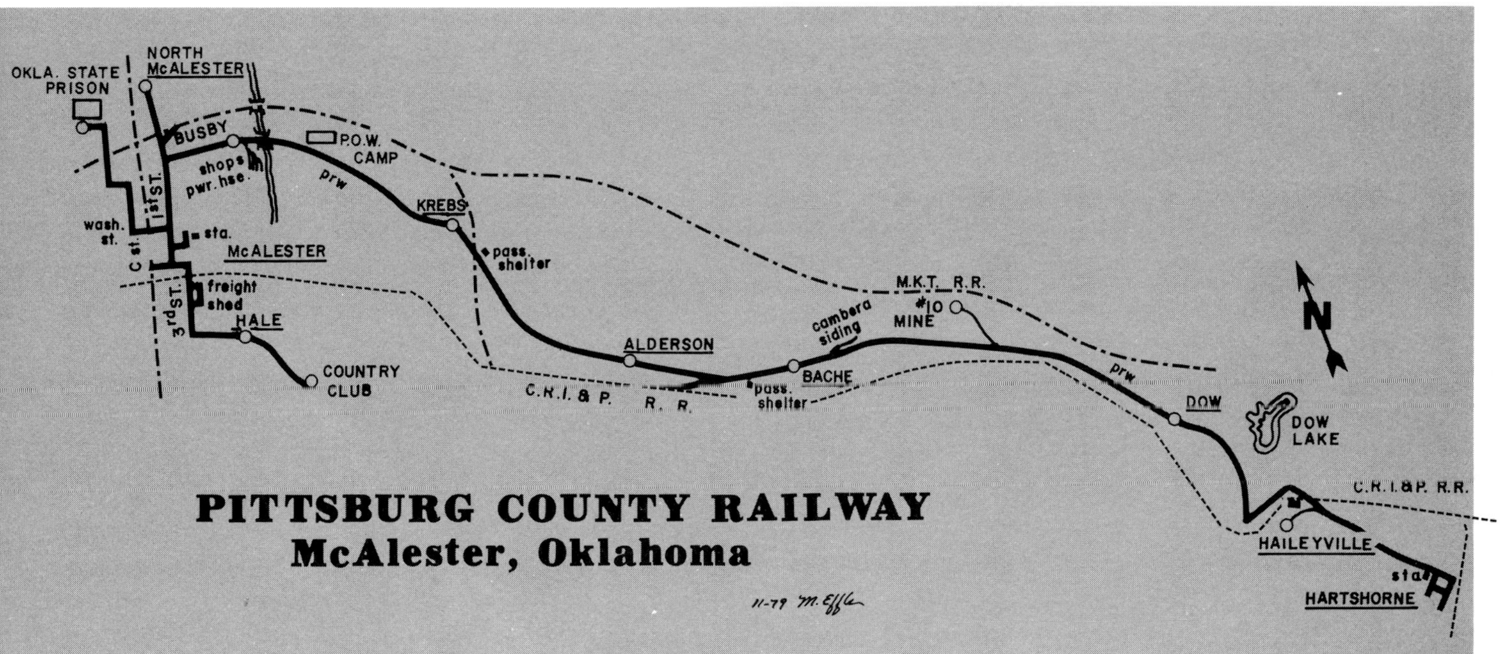

PITTSBURG COUNTY RAILWAY
McAlester, Oklahoma

TOP: Labeled for the Indian Territory Traction Co., the original McAlester company, mail and express car 26 is photographed at the American Car Co. factory in St. Louis, 1905.

Edward Watson Collection from Charles Smallwood

BOTTOM: Lightweight interurban 36 shows off double-diamond Pittsburg County emblem at the Busby barns, circa 1931.

C.J. DeVilbiss Collection

TOP: Elegance in steel and wood was this heavyweight Pittsburg County Railway interurban, number 32, taken at McAlester in 1932.
Stephen D. Maguire Collection

RIGHT: Locomotive 51 was used by Pittsburg County Railway to haul coal trains. *Texas ERA Collection*

MIDDLE: Efficient box motor 52 could carry packages, haul 10 loaded freight cars. *M.D. McCarter Collection*

TOP: Homely but utilitarian was Pittsburg County line car 48, shown at the Busby Shops on September 6, 1946.   *M.D. McCarter Collection*

ABOVE: One year before abandonment, Pittsburg County car 34 crosses the Dow Lake trestle, April 28, 1946.   *Ken Kidder, Magna Collection*

PITTSBURG COUNTY RAILWAY

FLEET NO.	BUILDER	ORDER	DATE	REMARKS
1-6	American	1129	6-7-18	ST Birney. New.
26	American	578	3-31-08	DT interurban combo. Reblt utility car 48.
30-31	Niles	340	1907	DT interurban combo. New.
32-33	?		1908	DT trailers.
34-35	Cincinnati	2535	1920	DT Lwt interurban. New.
36	Cincinnati	2560	1921	DT Lwt interurban. New.
51	?			Locomotive. Ex-Cincinnati & Columbus 1.
52	Cincinnati	2565	1921	Freight motor. New.

In 8/1918 had 16 passenger cars, 2 freight and 5 other.

Okmulgee Inter-Urban Railway

9. STREETCARS ON A SHOESTRING

ALTHOUGH Okmulgee has a history founded in the lore of the Creek Indians, its modern-day economy has been tied to minerals. It lies just south of the Creek County oil fields and north of some of eastern Oklahoma's oldest coal fields. The city itself boasted two glass plants which employed a sizable portion of its 15,000 population.

The name, Okmulgee, means "boiling water" and was brought by the Creek Indians from their ancient town of the same name in Alabama; the present city is on the site where the Creeks held some of their first councils after their forcible removal to the Indian Territory.

The village became the capital of the Creek Nation in 1868; in 1870 an intertribal council held at Okmulgee formulated a constitution for a proposed Indian state which was submitted to the different tribes for ratification. Alas, the constitution was never ratified, and the modern town was platted in 1900. As the new settlers moved in, the Creek governmental activities declined in importance.

The first rumblings of streetcar activity came in June 1907 when a franchise was issued by the city to the Electric Motor Railway. Nothing further was heard of this enterprise. Two years later, on June 7, 1909, a group including prominent local physician O.A. Lambert obtained a franchise for a streetcar line. Work began that same year, and the Okmulgee Inter-Urban Railway was capitalized at $200,000.

Dr. Lambert had moved his family to Okmulgee in 1907, the same year Oklahoma attained statehood. He continued to live in Okmulgee until his death in 1937, during which time he practiced medicine, edited a newspaper, entered the oil business, developed a residential area—with the help of his streetcars—named Lake Park, opened an amusement park and partly owned (and managed) a radio station.

Although the first leg of the system was to be a modest stretch of eight blocks, single track, from the principal downtown intersection of Sixth and Morton east to the Frisco depot, it took two years to begin operations. The first two cars, built by Pullman in 1895 and purchased second-hand from the Chicago City Railway Co., did not arrive until Sept. 1, 1910. Overflowing with enthusiasm, the *Okmulgee Democrat* on that date proclaimed that the cars had arrived "direct from the factory" in Chicago.

There were further difficulties, among them a dispute with the city over nonpayment of franchise taxes, and revenue service did not begin until around mid-November 1911, a full year after arrival of the "new" cars. Dr. Lambert held up operations for months in the hope he could get permission from the Frisco to cross its tracks and run a line to his Lake Park Addition which was developing residential lots. Another wrangle arose with wealthy residents along Morton St. (where Dr. Lambert hoped to lay tracks to reach the large glass plant southwest of town.)

Finally, around November 20, 1911, Dr. Lambert's street-cars began plying Sixth Street between downtown and the Frisco Depot. The Frisco was still resisting efforts to lay a crossing across its mainline tracks on Sixth, so the streetcar company announced early in 1912 it would extend to Lake Park anyway even if it meant passengers had to change cars at the railway crossing.

In March of that year Dr. Lambert finally won a legal battle with the residents of Morton St. and work began on the extension to the glass factory at Fourteenth St. and the Okmulgee Northern railroad tracks. In April the Frisco relented and the OI-U was permitted to cross the steam railway tracks; by late May both extensions were in service and Okmulgee had a streetcar line more than three and one-half miles in length.

On July 4, 1912, the OI-U took in some 4,000 fares at a nickel a ride from passengers carried to Dr. Lambert's Lake Park resort at the south end of Ohio Street in the east end of town.

It was not long before the public began complaining about Okmulgee's two streetcars, by then nearly two decades old, so on May 18, 1914, it was announced that Dr. Lambert and his superintendent, M.M. Simons, were leaving for St. Louis immediately to purchase two "new" streetcars. The cars were acquired, but did not stimulate business as Dr. Lambert had hoped.

In fact, on October 18 Simons threatened to cut service back from 20 minutes to every 40 minutes, discontinuing one of the two cars in operation. The OI-U had operated a 20-minute service all day, the two cars meeting on a passing track on Morton just south of Sixth. Simons' threat became reality only one month later, when the OI-U's one generator blew up. Repairs took several days, during which Okmulgee was without streetcar service altogether.

When on November 14 service was resumed, so few people wanted to ride that Simons put the one-car, 40-minute service into effect permanently.

Deteriorating tracks slowed the one car to an hourly headway in 1915, and, although there was at least one attempt to operate the second car, the service languished except when special events were held at Lake Park.

Nevertheless, in 1916 Dr. Lambert, still feuding with the residents along Morton St., announced he was going to rip up the tracks and relay them on Alabama St., three blocks west, so that his streetcars could continue to serve the glass plant. This immediately embroiled him in a three-way contest with the city and the Okmulgee Northern Railway, which wanted to lay its own track along Sixth St. west of Morton so that its gas-electric car to Henryetta could reach the center of Okmulgee.

Later, a compromise was announced under which both companies could use Sixth St., but Lambert was unable to raise the money to reroute the streetcars. Actually, dwindling patronage and the Model T auto were fast pushing the OI-U into insolvency. When the U.S. entered World War I in 1917, Lambert promptly enlisted as a YMCA volunteer and departed for the battlefields of France, leaving the struggling streetcar company to his brother, E.J. Lambert of Tulsa, as President and M.M. Simms as manager. The company's name was changed in 1918 to the Okmulgee Traction Co.

In either late 1919 or very early 1920, all service was abandoned, replaced for a time by the buses of the Okmulgee Street Transportation Lines. At least one of the buses towed a four-wheel trailer, highly novel for any U.S. bus system, then or now. The buses cost less to operate, but business was no longer to be had in a small city the size of Okmulgee and soon the bus line succumbed to paved streets and the private auto.

Shortly after the beginning of service, in late 1911 or early 1912, one of the original single-truck cars rumbles slowly down Sixth Street in downtown Okmulgee, the road to itself. *Leonida Kennedy Dalrymple Collection*

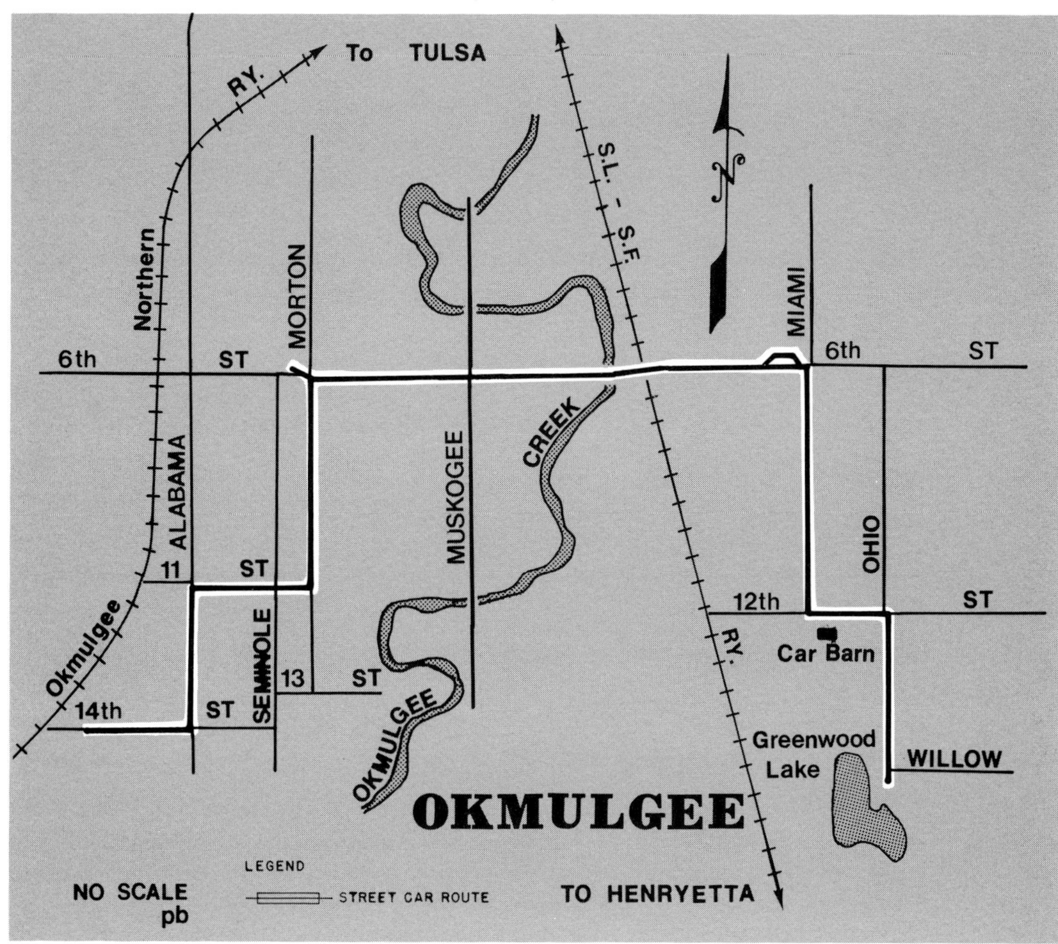

Okmulgee has a big city look about it in this photo, taken circa 1919. The two trolleys in the photo apparently were of the second group purchased in 1914. This view is in the collection owned by Mrs. George Knapp, granddaughter of the streetcar company's founder, Dr. O.A. Lambert.

Mrs. George Knapp Collection

After streetcar service ended, buses of the Okmulgee Street Transportation Co. took over. This 1920 view shows bus 4 and trailer with solid rubber tires. Operation of bus trailers, though common in Europe, has been very rare in the U.S. This Okmulgee experiment is especially unusual in that the traffic could hardly justify such high-capacity transit. The city has not had public transport of any type for decades now.
Traction Heritage from Stephen D. Maguire Collection

OKMULGEE INTER-URBAN RAILWAY

FLEET NO.	BUILDER	ORDER	DATE	REMARKS
(2 cars)	Pullman	836	7/1895	ST closed city. Acq. 1910 from Chicago City Ry. 2300,2316, ex-1899,1915.

In 8/1918 had 4 motor cars, one other. 3.5 miles of track.

10. TRACTION IN THE TERMINUS

WHEN THE Missouri, Kansas & Texas Railroad was built along the old Texas Trace through what became Eastern Oklahoma, at intervals along the way there were places colloquially called "terminuses" where the road ended for a time and trains were able to go only that far to bring loads of building materials, rails, ties—and settlers.

Boarding houses were set up and people gathered. Such a terminus through the summer of 1872 was the beginning of Muskogee, named after the Muscogee or Creek tribe of Indians. When the railroad resumed construction south, the principal activities moved on with the railroad, leaving only a collection of tents and shacks.

There was probably no reason for locating a town on the site of Muskogee until a new Indian agency building was located on a hill just northwest of those tents and shacks. Construction of this building was provided for in an 1866 treaty between the U.S. and the Creek Indians, their old building having been destroyed in the Civil War.

And so the cornerstone of this new agency building was laid on August 18, 1875, with appropriate ceremonies and the building was completed about January 1, 1876. The decision to locate the building at Muskogee was part of a plan to consolidate the different agencies of the Five Civilized Tribes into one agency, which functioned from then on as the Union Agency. Thus did Muskogee become, for a time, the most important city in the Indian Territory.

(It should be explained that, prior to statehood, what is now Oklahoma was for a time divided into two territories: Indian Territory, the eastern half, and Oklahoma Territory, the western half.)

Muskogee took on even more importance after creation by Congress on March 3, 1893, of the Dawes Commission to negotiate with the various Indian tribes looking toward creation of a state which would take over all the land within the Indian Territory. The Dawes Commission made Muskogee its headquarters, leading to incorporation of the town as a city on March 19, 1898.

Good transportation is important to any growing city, and Muskogee already had the main line of the Katy, a branch of the Frisco, and was very close to a line which would become a part of the Missouri Pacific. It also became a division point on the old Missouri, Oklahoma & Gulf Railway. But it had no city transportation.

This was remedied on May 14, 1904, when a franchise was granted to the Muskogee Electric Traction Co. which opened for service on March 15, 1905. It was the territory's third system to begin operations, after the Oklahoma City and McAlester lines. Originally the MET's capital stock was $300,000, later increased to $500,000.

Capt. Ira L. Reeves was president of the new company, with N.A. Gibson secretary and Louis K. Hyde, R.D. Benson and W.S. Benson the principal investors. The company became a part of the nationwide Byllesby syndicate at an early date. By 1909, it operated 16 motor cars plus four freight, mail and express cars over 14 miles of track. Power was obtained from the Muskogee Gas & Electric Co. Early growth was substantial; gross revenues mounted from $57,415 in 1906 to $72,365 in 1907 and $94,118 in 1908.

As elsewhere, the streetcars helped stimulate growth. The city's population rose from 4,254 in 1900 to 25,278 in 1910. In turn, the traction company continued to prosper, its revenues reaching $163,329 by 1911.

In that year the company's major traffic producer, the 10-mile interurban line to Fort Gibson, was constructed. A further 20-mile extension, to Tahlequah, was planned but never realized. Also in 1911 the small, independent Peoples Electric Railway, a storage battery line, was acquired.

By now the Muskogee Electric Traction owned 32 passenger cars plus one combination car, one electric locomotive and 11 work cars. Also listed on the company's roster in 1913 was a snow plow—making MET one of the southernmost streetcar systems to have one.

MET streetcar trackage attained its maximum in 1916, with 31 miles including the line to Fort Gibson which also served Bacone Indian College. Nineteen sixteen may have also marked Muskogee's high watermark in population, at 44,218. From then on the city's population maintained a slow but steady decline. It was after World War I that ridership on MET's streetcars leveled off, also, and declined even more rapidly than the city's population. A long and bitter

Purportedly the very first run on the Muskogee streetcar system was enacted in this photograph taken March 15, 1905. Gentlemen identified by circled numbers penned on the photo were (1) Tams Bixby, Muskogee newspaper publisher, and (2) Capt. Ira L. Reeves, president of the Muskogee Electric Traction Co.

A.F. von Blon—Texas ERA Collection

strike in 1919 did not help the MET's struggle to remain viable.

The company took the usual economy measures, including purchase of 12 single-truck Birney Safety Cars in 1922 and 1924, total conversion to one-man operation, and cutbacks in schedules. The Hyde Park and Fort Gibson lines brought in some freight revenue, but by the end of the decade only a 90-minute passenger headway was offered on these suburban runs.

Streetcar lines blanketed Muskogee pretty well, helped by its lack of physical growth in the 1920s. Principal services offered included the West Broadway, Fond du Lac, Hyde Park, East Okmulgee Ave., Fair Grounds, Midland Valley Shops, Monticello, Elgin Ave. and Reeves Addition lines, the latter built as late as 1912.

One handicap which the company never completely solved was the condition of the rickety Court Street bridge downtown which spanned the Katy Railroad tracks and connected the five West Side lines with the carbarn and the two suburban lines on the East Side. The bridge was old and in constant need of repair, and, toward the end, the city endured long interruptions of streetcar service because of problems with the span.

The Muskogee Electric Traction managed to outlive the Depression, but not as a streetcar operation. After only short notice, the entire streetcar system was abandoned on March 9, 1933, with the exception of the Fort Gibson tracks, retained until 1934 for freight service. The following morning, buses took over the West Broadway, East Okmulgee, Elgin Ave., Reeves Addition and Car Barn lines, following the trolley tracks almost exactly.

As a matter of fact, the Muskogee Electric Traction Co. continued to serve the public under that name, as a bus company, until a strike closed the company permanently in 1958.

Turner Hotel was one of Muskogee's principal early hostelries. An open car of the Muskogee Electric Traction Co. passes by on September 22, 1908.
Stephen D. Maguire Collection

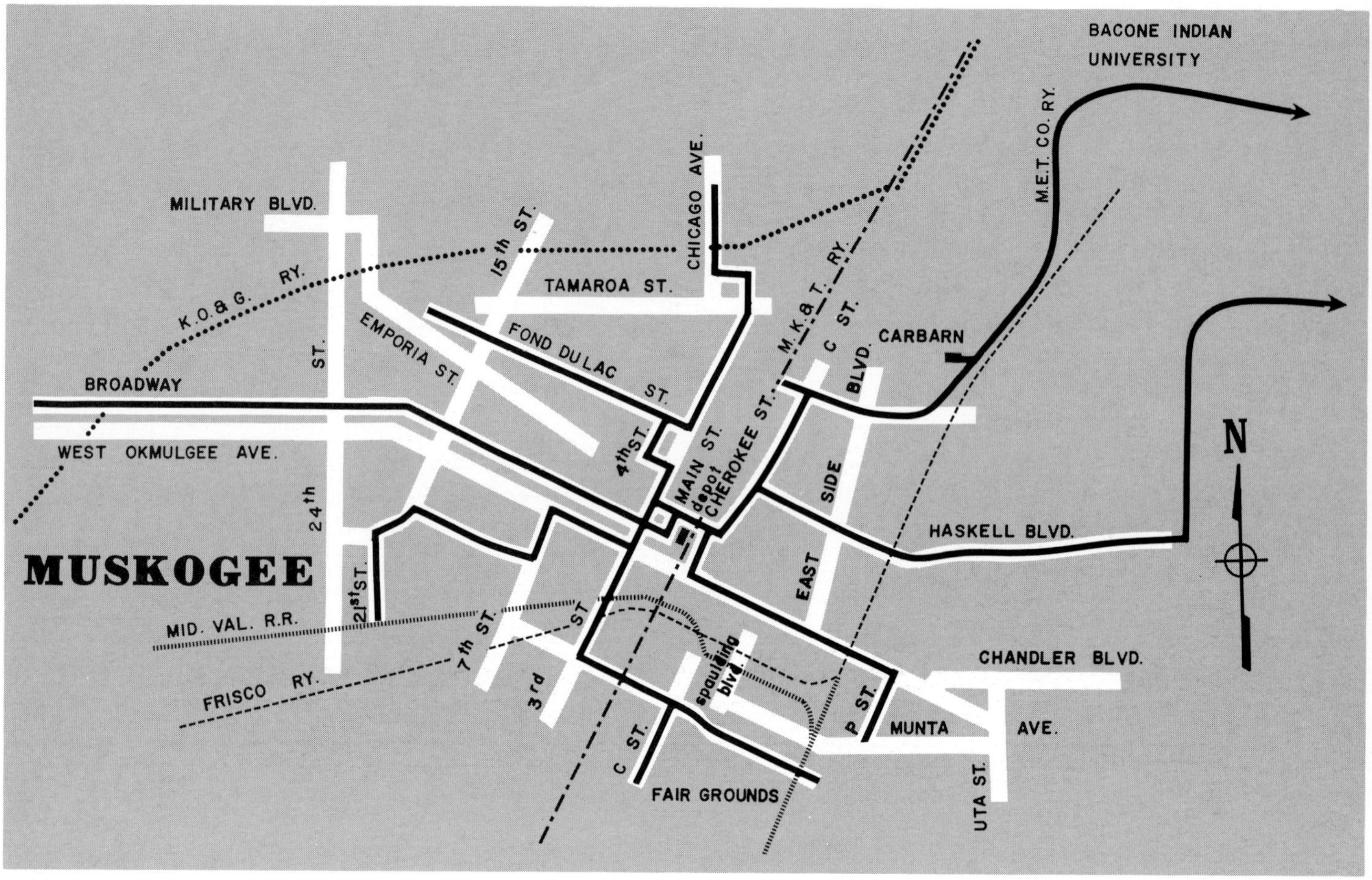

Battery car operated on the Peoples Electric Railway, an early line acquired by the MET and electrified.
Stephen D. Maguire Collection

TOP: Its new coat of varnish glistening, Muskogee car 51 displays its open platforms, later enclosed for protection against the elements.
Stephen D. Maguire Collection

BOTTOM: Ballast was nonexistent on the Fort Gibson line in the early days, but extra-long suburban car 110 with its maximum-traction trucks was taking it in stride.
C.J. DeVilbiss Collection

Single-truck, lightweight closed cars were the later standard on the MET; car 68 is shown in service, car 74 was photographed at the American Car Co. factory, 1912.   *Texas ERA Collection; Stephen D. Maguire Collection*

RIOTING IN MUSKOGEE.

Follows Attempt to Operate Street Car System.

[handwritten: June 20, 1919   Beggs Ind.]

Muskogee.—Street car service, resumed here after eleven days of idleness, was discontinued in the fear that violence which had marked the day would increase.

Mayor John L. Wisner telegraphed Lieutenant Governor Trapp requesting that the militia be called out. The acting governor refused to interfere at present.

Five conductors and motormen were badly beaten and stabbed by gangs of strike sympathizers. The men were taken from the cars at the ends of their runs and pummeled with iron pipe and stabbed. Three were carried to hospitals in serious condition.

Service was discontinued when crowds of strikers and sympathizers swarmed around the cars in the downtown districts threatening violence to the motormen and conductors. Traction company officials declared that bullets had been fired through the windows of two cars.

LEFT: Labor strife hit Muskogee's streetcar system following World War I. This June 20, 1919, newspaper clipping from the Beggs, Okla., *Independent* attests to the seriousness of the conflict. *Okla. Mount Spears Collection*

BELOW: This was typical Muskogee streetcar transfer; overprinted "2" designates day of month, in this case, January 2, 1922.

Stephen D. Maguire Collection

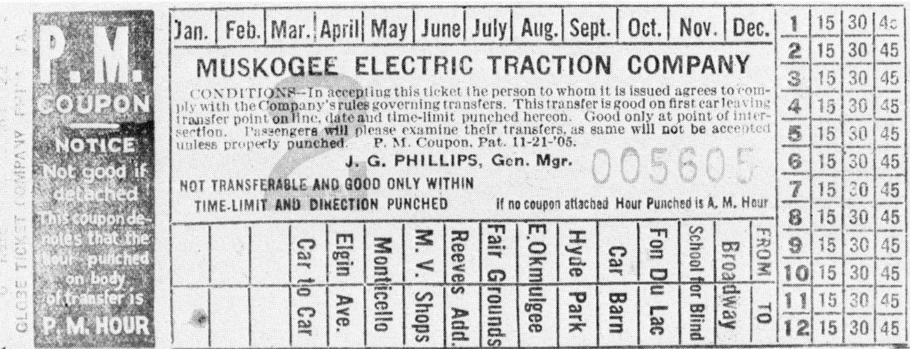

After long years of disuse, the carbarn of the Muskogee Electric Traction Co. was still standing northeast of the city.   *A.F. von Blon Collection from Stephen D. Maguire*

MUSKOGEE ELECTRIC TRACTION COMPANY

FLEET NO.	BUILDER	ORDER	DATE	REMARKS
(2 cars)	American	553	7-9-04	ST 10 bench open. New. Orig. blt for Manatee Lt & Tcn, FL but not del.
15	American	552	7-9-04	ST closed city. New. Orig. blt for Manatee Lt & Tcn, FL but not del.
27	American	611	11-23-05	DT interurban combo. New.
(4 cars)	Laclede			ST closed city. Acq 1905 United Rys & Elec (Baltimore) 2202,2203,2205, 2210; ex-City & Suburban 326,327,329,334; URE 1312,1313,1315,1320.
50-55?	Danville		1909	ST closed semiconvertible. New.
60-69?	American	917	12-15-11	ST closed semiconvertible. New.
100-109	American	952	11-9-12	DT closed city. New.
110-113	American	951	7-1-12	ST closed semiconvertible. New.
300-305	Cincinnati	2480	10/1922	ST Birney. New.
306-311	American	1370	3/11/24	ST Birney. New.
?	Plymouth	3445	4/1930	4-wheel gas/mech, loco. 25t, 127hp model HLB; acquired 6-15-33 from Plymouth; had been Commerce Sand & Gravel Co., Commerce, IA. Sold 8-17-60 Giant Portland Cement Co P-140, Harleyville SC.

Also had 2 work cars and one locomotive for use on the Ft. Gibson line.

PEOPLES ELECTRIC RY. CO. (Fort Gibson line)

1	Federal Stge Btry Co		1911	DT storage battery car, 40.6" long, an Edison-Beach car. Sold to Webbers Falls, Shawnee & Western RR, Webbers Falls OK, rblt w/gas engine.
?	McKeen		5/1911	Gas motor car; engine damaged and little used. Disp. unknown.

Sand Springs orphans' home was served directly by the yellow trolleys. Here is car 75 making its way through the home's campus en route to Tulsa, August 22, 1954.

William D. Middleton

11. WIDOWS, ORPHANS *and* INTERURBANS

RAILROADS and streetcar lines alike were built to make money, though some railroads and most streetcar lines became chronic failures in this endeavor. But few rail lines were set up as philanthropic institutions. The Sand Springs Railway was such a line, and not only did it succeed in making money, it succeeded in operating the last passenger streetcars in the state of Oklahoma.

That the Sand Springs Railway became such an economic success probably would not have been predicted back in 1911, when it was built primarily to serve an orphans' home lost in the sand hills some 10 miles west of Tulsa.

Charles Page struck it rich when he discovered the Taneha oil pool south of Tulsa. Prior to that time, Page had done just about everything; his colorful background included such diverse occupations as railroad station agent, chief of police, Pinkerton detective and Northern Pacific colonization agent.

With his newfound oil money, Page decided he wanted to be an industrialist. And, since he had a strong philanthropic bent, he jumped enthusiastically into a charitable cause that was to occupy him for the rest of his life.

In 1908 some Indians offered Page a 160-acre site along the Arkansas River west of Tulsa and near the village of Sand Springs which had once been used as a campground in the former Osage Indian Nation. Page bought it, and built his Sand Springs Home, for orphans and penniless widows.

The Katy Railroad served the area, but Page felt its infrequent steam-powered passenger trains would give poor service to his Home and to the townsite he was planning to develop at Sand Springs, which then numbered but 20 souls. So he built his own railway.

It is not certain that Page planned to operate the line by electricity at first, since he purchased and briefly operated a pair of 72-foot McKeen gasoline railcars on his new line, which linked the Home, Sand Springs and downtown Tulsa. At any rate, within a few months, electric wires had been strung and the first electric passenger cars were in service.

It was freight which quickly put the Sand Springs line into the profit column, and this was no accident. Oklahoma had finally achieved statehood in 1907, and Page believed that Oklahoma raw materials and fuel should be processed by Oklahoma labor to create new wealth for the Sooner State.

Controller on the brass, Sand Springs lightweight 75 wheels toward Sand Springs on trackage eminently suitable for heavy freight traffic.   *Magna Collection*

He set out to lure new industry along his line, and succeeded in locating the largest textile mill west of the Mississippi River, the only steel plant in Oklahoma, one of the few fruit jar and lamp chimney factories in the U.S., plus oil refineries, food-processing plants, machine shops and a thriving stockyards.

Much of this industrial and commercial complex was located right in Sand Springs, just a block or two away from the Katy Railroad, which had been asleep at the switch while Charles Page built.

Page did not overlook the needs of Sand Springs' hundreds of new residents. He built them an 80-acre park, a large zoo, a library, wide streets, and provided free building sites, cheap gas and cheap electricity.

Passenger and freight receipts from the railroad, plus royalties from 200 million cubic feet of gas fortuitously located on Page's lands surrounding Sand Springs, soon paid all the bills for the orphanage. The railroad continued to support Page's widows and orphans for decades.

By 1914 the population of Sand Springs had reached 2,000, and the Sand Springs Railway was humming with business. The Sand Springs park and zoo helped draw weekend visitors in droves—all on Page's trolleys. Eight electric interurban cars were furnishing passenger transportation, and a 50-ton electric locomotive was purchased from Westinghouse to replace steam power.

Passenger business continued to grow, and in 1916 the railway purchased two new 58-foot-long passenger cars and a pair of 60-footers followed in 1918. From then on, the company bought second-hand equipment and kept it in excellent condition at its well-equipped Sand Springs shops.

Page died in 1926, but the railroad kept right on supporting the Sand Springs Home. President T. H. Steffens, who replaced Page at the helm, was also one of the Home's original trustees. Freight service was stressed more and more, with carload freight interchanged with all four of Tulsa's mainline railroads: the St. Louis-San Francisco Railway, the Missouri-Kansas-Texas, the Midland Valley, and the Santa Fe.

Despite the onset of the Great Depression, the SS upgraded its passenger service in 1934 when it purchased seven lightweight 40-foot cars from the Cincinnati, Lawrenceburg & Aurora Railway of Ohio. Passenger fares remained at a nickel for a local ride and a dime for the full distance to Sand Springs and were not raised until 1953.

A year after the neighboring Oklahoma Union Railway closed out passenger service on its lines in 1933, the Sand Springs acquired its two double-truck Birney cars, numbering them 69 and 70, right after the ex-CL&A cars which were 62-68.

All through the 1930s the maroon Sand Springs cars rolled, seemingly immune from the ills which had killed all other rail passenger service in the Tulsa area. Service to Sand Springs was offered on a 20-minute headway all day long, with tripper cars to the suburban Bruner stop added in the rush hour to form a 10-minute headway to that point. Owl cars ran at hourly intervals.

Freight traffic reached a peak during World War II, largely due to expanded oil refinery operations. Oil traffic became far less important after the war when the large Sinclair Oil Co. plant, served exclusively by the SS, closed down. The Sand Springs line's energetic traffic sales department came to the rescue, and replaced the lost revenue with other business, much of it from new plants located along the main line.

The company pictured itself as a little giant among rail-roads. Track mileage totaled 36 miles in the postwar period, including 10.34 miles of main track, 5.36 miles of double track and 20.4 miles of sidings and spurs. For years, freight traffic averaged around 14,000 carloads yearly.

So intent was the line in its role as small-but-important freight feeder that it joined not only the American Short Line Railroad Assn. but the mighty Association of American Railroads as well.

The 1950s brought the Sand Springs Railway to a painful decision. Freight traffic was booming even more, with three regular freight crews kept busy operating a half-dozen Baldwin-Westinghouse electric locomotives. The original four units had proved to be insufficient to keep the freight cars moving, so in 1946 the SS bought two second-hand juice jacks from New York's Niagara Junction Railway.

Two-way radio was installed on locomotives for more effi-

Mainstay of Sand Springs Railway passenger operations in the late 1930s was a group of early lightweight cars acquired from the Cincinnati, Lawrenceburg & Aurora Railway. Notice that the rear door has been closed off with sheet metal, but will still open to permit ventilation for motorman.   *M.D. McCarter Collection*

TOP: It wasn't a palace, but the Sand Springs Railway's Tulsa waiting room provided not only shelter but snacks and cigarettes. Western Union was next door, complete with rack for messengers' bicycles. *Interurbans*

BOTTOM: Layover for cars on the Tulsa end was "Archer Alley," point where Sand Springs tracks foresook Archer St. for the Katy-Midland Valley freight interchange. If surroundings do not look exactly prosperous, fact was that the interurban came into town on the "wrong" side of the Frisco tracks and you had to walk several blocks to the business district. This didn't seem to hurt patronage, however. *Magna Collection*

cient dispatching of the crews. Despite such improvements, the company felt that the frequent passenger cars were delaying important freight movements despite the fact that much of the line was double track.

Not that the SS had neglected its riders. Passenger service had been modernized again, in 1947, with purchase of the Kansas Union Electric's fleet of double-truck Birneys, numbered 71-76. The Kansas line, which penetrated Oklahoma near its northeastern corner to serve Nowata, had just closed down and, although the six cars were in fairly battered condition, the Sand Springs shops effected a thorough reconditioning and the cars came out almost like new.

Nor was there complaint about passenger volume. More than one million passengers were handled annually, and these revenues constituted 20 percent of the Sand Springs Railway's gross revenue. But passenger service was increasingly expensive to operate, and President Steffens reckoned it was not paying its way. And, by the mid-1950s, trolley cars were becoming an anachronism, and no self-respecting, modern railroad wanted to have such museum pieces around.

A ride on a Sand Springs car at about this time was indeed a journey into the past—a most pleasant, agreeable past. Passengers boarded at the Sand Springs line depot on Archer Street and Boston Ave., just north of the main Tulsa business district. The line did not enter the main district, but a free shuttle bus was operated. The SS line's storefront depot was, in later years, something of an eyesore but the regular riders didn't seem to be bothered in the slightest.

Cars laid over a half block north where the track entered an alley. Boarding one of the large, yellow double-truck Birneys, the passenger settled down for a comfortable, swaying ride through Tulsa's industrial belt. After a few blocks of single-track street running, the car entered double track and private right-of-way briefly paralleling the Frisco, then swinging west in a graceful curve to follow the Arkansas River.

Passenger stops were frequent, first in the factory and warehouse district and then at the numerous residential subdivisions along the river. Several inbound Birneys were met, along with a freight movement or two. The motorman knew his regular customers, and said goodbye to them by name as they dropped off the yellow trolley, one by one.

Rolling westward, the car passed the stockyards, then entered a brief section of open country paralleling the Katy Railroad Osage subdivision. At Lake Station, an electrified track crossed the Katy and headed for the hills to the northwest; this was the return line of a large, one-way loop taken by the passenger cars through Sand Springs.

Then the car reached the SS line's shops and yard at the east edge of Sand Springs, where much industrial trackage diverged. Turning sharply to the right, the car entered the

Outbound Sand Springs car negotiates the single-track portion of Archer St. Turnout in the foreground was the beginning of double track which extended all the way to Sand Springs. *Texas ERA Collection*

With double track ending at this point, inbound 71 awaits outbound car before proceeding the last few blocks
to the station. Circa 1946.
Interurbans

Viaduct leading to Tulsa's mainline Union Station is just visible to the right of car 70, while far down Archer St. is a
Tulsa City Lines Twin Coach city bus, circa 1938.
Magna Collection

main downtown street of Sand Springs on single track, stopping at the modest brick passenger station.

Returning to Tulsa, the car passed the Charles Page Library, took another right turn and headed through the pleasant, wooded grounds of the Sand Springs Home and park. Another mile or two of meandering single track brought the car back to the main line at Lake Station. After a safety stop at the Katy diamond, the car edged across the Katy and onto the "wrong" SS line double track until a crossover was reached a few yards further on.

All along, passengers boarded and alighted, and acted generally as if the service was good, dependable and might last forever.

Which, alas, was not to be the case. In late 1954 the decision was taken not only to cease passenger operations, but all electric operation as well. On January 2, 1955, at 6 A.M., the last revenue passenger car of the Sand Springs Railway tied up. A ceremonial "last run" with several of the yellow trolleys was held several days later, but an era was at an end. Another company's buses took over the passenger duties, and the passenger cars were scrapped.

Within a few months, electric freight operation was ended as well, two of the company's 50-ton locomotives being sold to the Tulsa-Sapulpa Union Railway. Three diesels provided motive power and the freight business continued to prosper as before.

In fact, by 1975 the Sand Springs Railway, still fiercely independent, was pouring record profits into the Sand Springs Home, which continued to own 100 percent of the road's stock. Sand Springs had grown to 14,000 residents and freight revenues in 1974 were up 30 percent from the previous high.

The parallel Katy did not fare nearly as well, its right-of-way truncated by a new reservoir. After the trolleys ceased to run, the passengers seemed to drift away. Auto traffic along the four-lane Charles Page Blvd. increased markedly, while the Sand Springs buses ran nearly empty. Eventually, Sand Springs lost its bus service, although the city bus system today maintains service as far west as Bruner.

Still, the Sand Springs Railway endures, doing what it does best—hauling freight, keeping alive the legend of Charles Page, and supporting countless widows and orphans.

Beauty of the summer Oklahoma countryside is evident in this shot near Sand Springs Park and starring car 65, one of the Cincinnati lightweights.

Interurbans

Freight yard to the left collected cars for the nearby Frisco interchange. Well-kept passenger tracks are to the right, and feel the weight of inbound car 75 on a balmy 1954 summer day.   *William D. Middleton*

TOP: Mid-Continent oil refinery provides the backdrop, across Arkansas River, as an inbound Sand Springs car takes the gentle curve toward downtown Tulsa. *William D. Middleton*

BOTTOM: Shortly after leaving Archer St., Sand Springs line's double track made a sweeping curve alongside the Arkansas River where a small freightyard was located. This is a short-turn Bruner car. *William D. Middleton*

TOP: A stop at the Sand Springs Sanatorium also was a feature of every trip.   *Interurbans*

BOTTOM: Main Street in suburban Sand Springs carried single-track streetcar loop line, past the Charles Page Library (mostly obscured by car 73) and around to Charles Page Park and Hospital. Every 20 minutes a car for Tulsa would rumble by, day and night.

Texas ERA Collection

September 8, 1948

Mr. Ira L. Swett, Editor & Publisher
Interurbans
1414 South Westmoreland Avenue
Los Angeles 6, California

Dear Mr. Swett:

Thank you for yours of August 23, together with the complimentary issue of INTERURBANS which I read with a great deal of interest especially the article about the Sand Springs Railway of course.

I will send you some photographs of these cars together with a brief description. They have all been reconditioned and painted a bright yellow. The Sand Springs Railway Co. has a distinction of being owned by an Orphans Home and the net profit with other income was left to the Orphans Home by the late Charles Page to endow it and I presume that the only line that is so owned. Here is a little booklet titled "Unto The Least Of These" about the Sand Springs Home that provides a home of families of orphan children to keep the sisterhood and brotherhood together as well as a colony for widowed mothers with children that they could be cared for. The children go to public school, they attend a church of their own faith, and are raised under an atmosphere of home life in the regular American way. We accept no outside charity or gifts and it was established in 1908.

I mention this because so many lines are owned by many stockholders but the Sand Springs Railway has a unique distinction.

Very truly yours,

T. H. Steffens
President

S/fj

Cooperative attitude of Sand Springs Railway employees, from President T. H. Steffens on down, is amply demonstrated by this letter from Steffens to Ira L. Swett of Interurbans back in 1948. Railroad's keen interest in the orphans' home is also shown in the letter. *Interurbans*

Interplay between the Sand Springs line and the St. Louis-San Francisco Railway is demonstrated at the Frisco interchange near downtown Tulsa. Electric motor 1002 pulls up alongside Frisco switcher 273 on the SLSF Tulsa-Oklahoma City mainline.
William D. Middleton

Locomotive 1006 tugs a cut of tank cars from the Sinclair Oil plant. Unfortunately Sinclair closed down its refinery after World War II.
William D. Middleton

LEFT: Passenger line of Sand Springs Railway is momentarily tied up as electric locomotive 1002 switches a boxcar and some gondolas filled with steel scrap. Frisco mainline is adjacent.
William D. Middleton

BELOW: Freight paid the bills and kept the widows and orphans happy on the Sand Springs line. Here is Baldwin-Westinghouse juice jack 1003 performing switching chores in the Sand Springs area, 1947.
Interurbans

Early Sand Springs rolling stock, acquired in 1911 and 1912, was classic in design. Wooden trailer 102 (top) was built in 1911 by the Danville (Ill.) Car Co. and was likely converted later into motor car 33. Car 31 (middle), shown at the American Car Co. plant, was delivered in June of 1912. Right: Interurban 37, one of the heaviest cars the line ever owned, was photographed in Sand Springs and arrived in 1911.

Two: Texas ERA Collection;
Edward B. Watson Collection,
from Charles Smallwood

Just minutes from downtown Tulsa, Sand Springs Railway car 67 ambles down Archer St. with a standing load of passengers, 1948.
Gordon Zahorik

The dust held down by a fresh spring rain, Sand Springs car 62 drifts along Archer St. in Tulsa, past the SS freight station (see emblem on building immediately left of car). The year was 1946, and the dark maroon paint scheme was about to give way to a new bright yellow, coincident with arrival of "boomer" cars from the Union Electric Railway in Kansas.
M.D. McCarter Collection

RIGHT: This express motor, built by Brill, was acquired from the Philadelphia & West Chester Traction Co. Its use on the Sand Springs Railway was marginal after the mid-1930s. *Magna Collection*

BELOW: Cincinnati-built car 23 dated to 1915, but remained on the property for years after departure of the other early cars. In fact, it held down the Sand Springs "owl" run until after World War II. Car 41, shown behind the barn years after retirement (note missing trolley poles) is an example of what the road's own shop forces could do. It was one of three motor cars built in Sand Springs in 1917 and 1918.

Interurbans; Stephen D. Maguire Collection

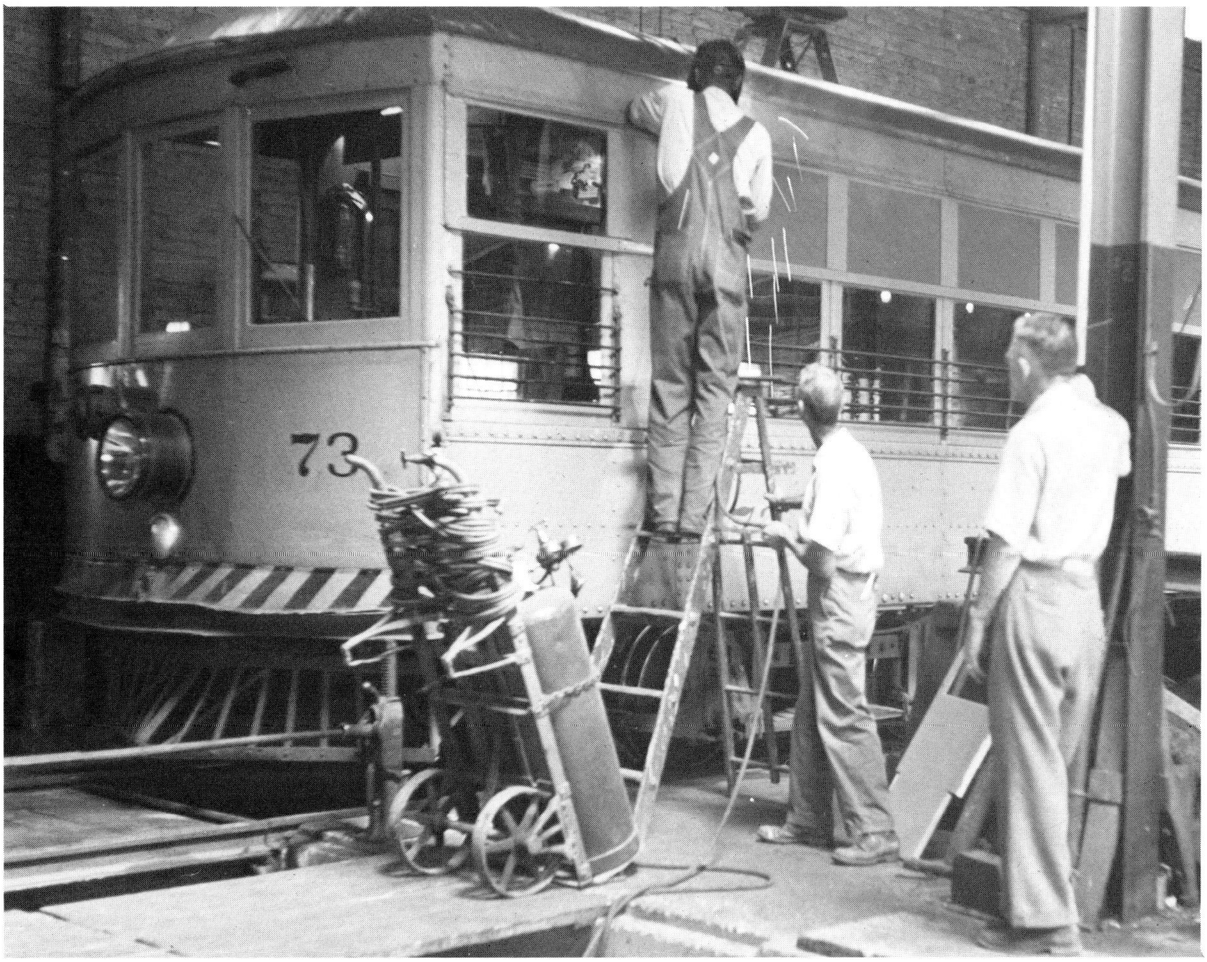

TOP: Well-equipped barn and shops could do just about anything for Sand Springs line rolling stock, including building it from scratch. Here's the yard circa 1937; the two lightweight cars at right were hand-me-downs from neighboring Tulsa-Sapulpa interurban. *Laurence Veysey Collection*

MIDDLE: Minor repair job occupies Sand Springs shopmen. This photo was taken only three months prior to the end of all passenger service in 1955. *William D. Middleton*

RIGHT: Maintenance on the Sand Springs was always of a high order. Here is line car A-4 and crew repairing the trolley wire near Sand Springs, 1947. *Ira L. Swett*

SAND SPRINGS INTERURBAN RY. CO.

FLEET NO.	BUILDER	ORDER	DATE	REMARKS
1	McKeen		4/1911	Sold 1912 Riviera Beach & Westn 101; adv for sale 6/1919; car was seen in Houston junkyard lettered Roby & Nor but R&N never owned it.
2	McKeen	103	4/1911	Sold 1916 Midland Valley 2; resold 4/1925 Union Pacific M-6.
101	Danville	565	1911	Express tlr. Rblt as express motor 7?
102-103	Danville	566	1911	Closed psgr tlrs. Both reblt as motor cars 33,35.

In February, 1914, also owned 3 steam locomotives.

SAND SPRINGS RAILWAY CO.

FLEET NO.	BUILDER	ORDER	DATE	REMARKS
17,19,21,23	St Louis	?	?	Trailers, pur. 2nd hand 1913. Sold 1917.
21,23 (2nd)	Cincinnati	1945	1915	DT interurban. Blt as Cushing Tcn Co 1-2, never used there and delivered to SS. No. 1-2 until 1917 when re# 21,23.
25,27	?	?	1912	DT open cars, motors. Ex? Very large cars, had Brill 27E1 trucks.
29,31	American	941	6-17-12	DT closed interurban.
33,35	Danville	566	1911	DT closed interurban. Reblt 1913-14 from trailers 102,103.
37	Kuhlman	505	1911	DT closed city cars. Probably diverted at factory, not delivered.
37 (2nd),39	Co. shops		1917	DT combo interurban. Probably 2nd hand cars reblt by SS; may have been trailers when acquired.
41,43	Co. shops		1923	DT closed interurban. Probably 2nd hand cars reblt by SS.
45	Co. shops		1923	DT closed interurban. Probably 2nd hand car reblt by SS.
51,53,55, 57,59,61	?	?	?	DT trailers. Acquired 1918, ex?

On 12/18/1924 a carhouse fire destroyed 14 passenger cars, 1 express car and 1 loco. Cars 21,25,27,29,33,39,43,45,51, 53,55,57,61 were lost. Loco and express car have not been identified. Roster after carhouse fire follows:

FLEET NO.	BUILDER	ORDER	DATE	REMARKS
22,24	American	794	1909	DT interurban combine. Acq. 1925 from Arkansas City-Winfield Nor.Ry, ex-Southwestern Interurban, KS. Orig. Joliet & Sou Tcn Co 117-121 ser.
23	Cincinnati	1945	1915	DT interurban. Blt as Cushing Tr Co 2.
26,28,30	St Louis	930	4-20-12	DT interurban. Acq. 1925 from Union Tcn Co. KS 40,42,44.
31	American	941	6-12-12	DT interurban.
35	Danville	566	1911	DT interurban. Orig. trailer 103.
37	Co. shops		1917	DT interurban combo. Probably 2nd hand trailer motorized by SS.
41	Co. shops		1923	DT interurban. Probably 2nd hand car reblt by SS.

In 1933, cars 22,26,31,35,37 were scrapped; replaced by the CL&A cars. This left only car 23 of the original cars.

FLEET NO.	BUILDER	ORDER	DATE	REMARKS
62-68	Cincinnati	2290	1917	DT lightweight interurban. Acq. 1932 Cincy Lawrenceburg & Aurora 915-921.
69-70	American	1148	9-3-18	DT lightweight interurban. Acq. 1934 from Okla Union Ry. 107-108.
71-76	American	1395	5-18-25	DT lightweight interurban. Acq. 1947 from Union Elec Ry KS 71-75,70.

When 71-75 were obtained, cars 62-67 were scrapped.

FLEET NO.	BUILDER	ORDER	DATE	REMARKS
7	Danville	565	1911	Express motor. Rblt from trailer 101? Retired 1925.
8	Brill	20412	1917	Express motor. Acq. 1925 from Phila & West Chester Tcn. 08.
1001	Baldwin-West.	41053	12/1913	50t B-B elec. loco. New. Scrapped 1956.
1002	Baldwin-West.	41893	2/1915	50t B-B elec. loco. Blt as Cushing Tcn Co. 501 but del. to SS. Sold 1956 to T-SU 1002.
1003	Baldwin-West.	48752	5/1918	50t B-B elec. loco. New. Scrapped 1956.
1004	Baldwin-West.	60537	6/1928	50t B-B elec. loco. New. Sold 1956 to T-SU 1004.
1005	Baldwin-West.	53027	2/1920	43t B-B elec. loco. Acq. 3/1946 Niagara Jct 6. Scrapped 1956.
1006	Baldwin-West.	53050	2/1920	43t B-B elec. loco. Acq. 3/1946 Niagara Jct. 7. Scrapped 1956.
100	EMD	20891	2/1956	SW900 B-B diesel loco. New.
101	EMD	20892	2/1956	SW900 B-B diesel loco. New.
102	EMD	23782	7/1957	SW900 B-B diesel loco. New.

12. BLACK GOLD _and_ TROUBLED TROLLEYS

SAY THE WORD "Tulsa" and the world immediately thinks of oil—wooden derricks, brawling roughnecks, boom times and the black gold which turned America into a nation of cars, trucks and paved highways. Indeed, Tulsa has always billed itself as the "oil capital of the world" and over the years has boasted of several major refineries and oil corporate headquarters.

Yet Tulsa, a city of modest size during the early oil booms, offered three competitive electric railway systems battling for the public's nickel. One—the Sand Springs Railway—ran passenger streetcars as late as 1955 and still exists as a profitable freight railroad. A second—Oklahoma Union Railway—gave up passenger cars early but continues to this day with a vestigial freight service.

The third system—the Tulsa Street Railway—emerged as the biggest passenger carrier in town. It was also the unluckiest. The system was never profitable, its lines never kept up with the city's population growth, its cars were shabby, and indeed the line was nearly stillborn at the beginning. TSR was Oklahoma's major hard-luck story in electric railroading.

Perhaps the trouble was that Tulsa was simply too small to support three street railway companies. True, the Sand Springs line was technically an interurban whose yellow double-truck Birneys were but a sideline to its thriving carload freight business, but it served one of Tulsa's major public transportation corridors. Which is why its owners found it economic to continue passenger service long after trolleys had vanished from all other Oklahoma cities.

The OUR line, connecting Tulsa and nearby Sapulpa, was also an interurban but a major source of its income in passenger days came from its one crosstown route from Red Fork, across the Arkansas River from Tulsa, through downtown Tulsa and out East 11th to the Fair Grounds. This also was a major transit corridor and one denied to the struggling TSR.

In consequence, Tulsa Street Railway, hedged in by its two rivals, harassed by disgruntled patrons and (in the view of its critics) mismanaged, became one of the first rail systems gobbled up by the bus-minded National City Lines which for the first time gave Tulsa a citywide transit system —one on rubber tires, and burning a hometown product— gasoline.

Today, Tulsa is Oklahoma's second-largest city, nosed out by Oklahoma City, the state capital. But back in 1905 when Tulsa had but 4,000 souls, there was some question of whether Tulsa or nearby Sapulpa was going to become Eastern Oklahoma's major metropolis. In 1900, Tulsa's population numbered a scant 1,350, hardly enough people to support any kind of public transportation. The oil boom was dawning, and many of those in the know were betting on Sapulpa, 12 miles south.

A typical attitude is related in Lewis Meyer's hilarious book about his father, Max Meyer, a pioneer Sapulpa merchant, entitled *Preposterous Papa* (World Publishing Co., 1959) that offers a revealing contrast in the brand of boosterism displayed by the two rival towns. In one passage, Max explains to his children why he decided to settle in Sapulpa:

"Well," said Papa, "it (Sapulpa) wasn't always smaller than Tulsa. When your great-grandfather Philip Levy gave me my pick of towns in Oklahoma I chose Sapulpa because it looked like the winner of the two towns. Sapulpa was the division point and headquarters of the Frisco Railroad. Sapulpa was smack dab in the middle of the Glenn pool, the biggest oil strike in history! Why, in 1906, when Philip Levy built my store for me, Sapulpa was bigger than Tulsa."

"What happened?"

"Nobody knows for sure. We built a big electric sign over the highway comin' into town. It had lights in ten colors, and it proclaimed: *Sapulpa, The Oil City of the Southwest!* And while we were buildin' that sign Tulsa was buildin' a five-story luxury hotel where the oilmen could sleep in comfort and do their lease tradin' in the lobby . . . the minute that hotel was built, Tulsa started passin' us. . . ."

And so Tulsa was on the road to prosperity, and needed a streetcar line. It soon had more than it bargained for.

In 1905 eighteen Tulsa businessmen organized the Tulsa Street Railway Co. to build the city's first rail line. Among the incorporators were L.M. Poe, James G. Gillette, J.J. Hall, Al Friend, L.D. Marr, Don Hagler and George Wil-

No streetcars are in sight in this 1907 view of Main Street. Reason: cars haven't started operating and the overhead is only partly in place.
Howard Hopkins Collection

liamson — none of whom had ever been in the transportation business. Nevertheless, Tulsa's city fathers immediately regarded the group as potential robber barons and the city council placed such stiff terms on the proposed franchise that no bank would finance the venture.

Frustrations mounted. Muskogee, Oklahoma City, Enid, Shawnee and McAlester already had streetcars. How could anybody take Tulsa seriously as an oil capital — or any kind of capital — if it did not even provide its citizens with the means to move about? The fact that Oklahoma still had not attained statehood and was still known as the Indian Territory placed another roadblock in the way, because potential Eastern financial backers were wary of the territory's well-known hostility toward large corporations. Then — as now — legislators ranted against "unjust" freight rates levied against farmers by the Eastern capitalists.

At the same time, there was open warfare between local city councils and utility companies — gas, electricity and water. Tulsa's city government regarded the infant Tulsa Street Railway as another of this rapacious breed. When Poe made a trip to Chicago to get financing for the new line he was bluntly told that no capitalist would put a dime into the Indian Territory.

Then along came C.H. Bosler of Dayton, Ohio, a minor-league traction magnate who had started the Enid streetcar system. He was a born organizer and, when put in charge of the company, was able to hammer out an acceptable franchise with the city. Acceptable, that is, if he could begin laying rails within 60 days.

Bosler's original plans called for tracks on Main Street from 10th Street north to the Katy railroad tracks (at Cameron St.) plus a line east and west on Fifth Street from Lawton Ave. to Madison Ave., altogether about two miles of route. While still waiting for rails to lay, Bosler in mid-1906 made a shrewd deal to extend his not-yet-built line further east to the Lynch-Forsythe and Gillette-Hall additions in return for $10,000 and 15 percent of the lot sale. This infusion of cash helped speed things up considerably.

Summer, 1906, turned into Fall and still no new rails appeared from the East. With his 60-day deadline for track-laying fast approaching, Bosler borrowed two rails from the Frisco Railway and spiked them into place near First and Main streets. Although Bosler had technically complied with the franchise, the rails were a nuisance to horse and wagon traffic and his men quickly covered them over.

Actual construction finally commenced early in 1907. Operations were supposed to start before June 1 according to the franchise, but again Bosler faced a crisis: he had no rolling stock. New cars were on order, but were delayed at the factory. Negotiations with the Boston Elevated Railway for a trio of single-truck open electric cars were under way, but time was short.

And so with the city council breathing down his neck, Bosler went to Muskogee, rented a streetcar from that system, loaded it on a flatcar and had it shipped to Tulsa. On May 27, 1907, the very last day he could begin operations or forfeit the franchise, Bosler's rented streetcar traversed his Fifth Street rails from one end to the other — hauled by two sturdy mules. The electric wires had not yet been erected.

This token gesture apparently was enough to satisfy the city, for Bosler was allowed to complete his line, take delivery of four new cars (two open, two closed) and begin revenue service in July, with Mayor W. E. Rohde, members of the city council and representatives of the press aboard

Newfangled trolleys had not been in operation long when this 1908 photo was taken at Third and Main, looking south. Car 105 is an open breezer, very popular in days gone by.   *George Howard from Stephen D. Maguire Collection*

the first car. Tulsa had now taken its place alongside Muskogee, Oklahoma City, Enid and McAlester as a streetcar town.

The new service was welcomed by Tulsans, and from opening day until the end of the year the TSR counted 336,600 passengers and took in $17,186 in gross revenue. By October of 1907, the company offered a 10-minute headway on the North Main Street and West Fifth Street lines, and 15-minute service on the South Main and the Third Street line.

TSR was not to enjoy its monopoly on local electric rail-

ABOVE: By 1909, Tulsa had gotten bigger and the trackage on Main Street had been partially doubled. Horses were still the main form of motive power. *Beryl D. Ford Collection*

RIGHT: Builders photo of Tulsa Street Railway car 205 was taken at the American Car Co. St. Louis factory in 1908. TSR followed the unusual practice of numbering its vehicles by fives (e.g., 200, 205, 210 were consecutively numbered cars). This idea may have been brought to Tulsa by C.H. Bosler, company president, from his hometown of Dayton where it was also employed. *Texas ERA Collection*

way transportation for long. In 1909 a charter was granted to a rival group headed by Albert A. Small for the Oklahoma Union Traction Co., which petitioned the city for a franchise covering streets not used by TSR. With but one dissenting vote, the council gave its blessing.

OUT especially wanted to build a line linking Owen Park, on the city's west end just north of the Katy Railroad tracks, with Orcutt Lake located at what is now 18th Street and St. Louis—the present Swan Lake. This route was to traverse downtown Tulsa via Fourth Street (halfway between the TSR lines on Third and Fifth) and reach the lake via Elgin Street and East 11th. This area was already built up, and TSR had done nothing to serve it.

With approval for the line secured from the city and construction crews at work on the OUT line, the TSR reacted. Quickly, a third car was added to the TSR East First line and on July 1, 1909, that company announced that the East First line would be extended to Kendall College, at East Seventh and Delaware. The wily Bosler managed to finance this extension with a bonus of $6,000 from the Tulsa Commercial Club. Meantime, he convinced the city council to deny a competing application from OUT for a line to the college.

Three new and one used streetcars arrived on the TSR property in 1909 as the two companies girded for battle. Service on the OUT line to Orcutt Lake began on December 22, 1909, with a large crowd turning out for the festivities. The next year, the TSR was building two more extensions, one on South Main from 13th to17th, and the other a rival line to Owen Park via West Third.

OUT also wanted to use West Third for its Owen Park line, and the two companies talked of a construction "race" to the West Third overpass over the Frisco Railway. The battle turned to the city council which, on March 22, awarded the West Third franchise to TSR. Oklahoma Union appealed to the courts, but lost.

The feud only got hotter. OUT announced it was going to build an interurban all the way to Sapulpa, 16 miles south, and a $300,000 construction contract for this line was awarded in November of 1910.

There followed months of delicate negotiations with the TSR, which wasn't interested in building any interurban lines. In February 1911, TSR agreed to let OUT cross its Owen Park tracks twice to reach the bridge across the Arkansas River to West Tulsa, and thence to Sapulpa. And the OUT was permitted to build a branch to Owen Park as well.

Four more cars, single-truck semi-convertibles, were pur-

Business is booming in Tulsa, circa 1909, with buildings under construction everywhere. This is Third and Main, looking north past TSR car.
Charles Smallwood Collection

TOP: Horseless carriages bar the way of this southbound Tulsa Street Railway open car, 1910. The Tulsa Motor Car Co. showrooms are out of picture to left, and the photographer needed the whole street to capture this snappy lineup. Soon, the auto would mean financial trouble for the trolleys, too.   *Beryl D. Ford Collection*

BOTTOM: Third and Main was traditionally the busy "trolley corner" in Tulsa. Here we see car turning left from Third to North Main while two westbound cars board passengers across street. Hotel Tulsa is in background. The year is 1914.
                    Beryl D. Ford Collection

New Hotel Tulsa towered above Tulsa Street Railway single-trucker on Third Street, 1914. Second trolley is about two blocks in the distance. Shortly afterward, this line was double-tracked.
Beryl D. Ford Collection

chased from Barney & Smith in 1910 as TSR added another line, on South Frisco from Fifth to Fifteenth. By 1912 trackage on the TSR measured 11 miles, with 17 streetcars in revenue service plus six trailers, the latter acquired secondhand from a line in Upper New York State. The barn and shops were located at 747 West Fifth Street.

When the Owen Park line was completed, it was linked up with a new line on the east end of the system — the Bellview route which diverged from the Kendall College trackage at East Third and Madison and reached 15th and Quincy. This was a direct invasion of the Oklahoma Union's Orcutt Lake territory; the new TSR line crossed the OUT line at East 11th and Quincy and then ran two blocks parallel to it to the end of the line.

Oklahoma Union's answer was to build a line further out East 11th to the Kendall College area, although for the most part it served new territory and did not parallel the TSR college line. This OUT line eventually reached the state fairgrounds, far beyond the end of the TSR tracks.

April 1912 marked the inauguration of Tulsa's third electric line — the Sand Springs Railway. Although the line to the suburb of Sand Springs, seven miles west of downtown Tulsa, had been opened for business the previous year with a pair of McKeen gasoline cars, the traffic soon became too heavy for this experimental type of propulsion.

The Sand Springs line's impact on the fortunes of TSR were negligible, since it served an area just opening up. Yet, had TSR seen the possibilities of this area first, or in some manner merged with the Sand Springs line later, its financial health would have been immeasurably stronger.

At any rate, by 1915 TSR was operating 22 passenger and two work cars, and was meeting a monthly payroll of $3,626 including $1,634 for motormen and $699 for conductors. Six routes were operated, the fare was 5 cents (children's tickets were only two and a half cents) and policemen, firemen and postmen were carried free if in uniform.

The system's "best" line, Main Street, had been extended on the south to 18th Street and on the north to Cameron Street, where it jogged west two blocks to Denver. The line then continued on North Denver to Pine Street. TSR bought a bus, too, to serve West Tulsa in competition with the OUT's Sapulpa interurban cars.

The year 1915 was profitable for TSR. Conductors and motormen were paid 22 cents an hour at the start (veterans made 26 cents) and the firm's net earnings for the year were $40,442.71. In 1916 the profit shot up to $84,049. The disruptions of World War I and its resulting inflation rapidly changed the company's rosy outlook, and soon the battle turned to one attempting to stem a tide of red ink.

This development came despite a rapidly booming Tulsa

North and South Main Street drew the company's only modern double-truck cars. Here's a homeward-bound crowd boarding at Third Street.
C.J. DeVilbiss Collection

population. The city had some 40,000 residents in 1915 but by 1920 this had risen to 80,000. Big money was pouring into the oil fields, and refineries and tank farms were springing up everywhere. The Tulsa skyline began to rise. Black gold was the topic of every conversation, and the smell of money was in the air.

All of which began to put a terrific strain on the city's streetcar system. TSR bought five modern double-truck cars in 1917 for the Main Street line, and followed that up in 1918 with its first order of six single-truck Birney cars, an economy model which saved on power and weight and also permitted one-man operation.

TSR did the best it could. Its operations probably attained a peak around August of 1923, when system trackage reached 21 miles, and the company listed 52 cars in the fleet (many of which were probably in storage). To open up territory beyond the end of the tracks—and by 1923 there was a lot of it—the TSR operated 23 newly purchased buses. Cash fare was up to 7 cents, with four tickets available for 25 cents.

One problem was the jitney bus, which had appeared on Tulsa streets in the Spring of 1920. The jitney craze had started in California in 1913 and spread to nearly every sizable city which operated streetcars. The jitney got its name because of the 5-cent (a "jit") fare generally charged by the owner-driver of the "jitney" car, usually a Ford Model T. Many cities eventually banned jitneys by law, since they tended to siphon off the cream of a streetcar company's traffic, but in Tulsa the jitneys endured until 1928 when the TSR lowered its fares to 5 cents to meet the competition.

The real villain in Tulsa, as elsewhere, was the private auto, and in 1925 with paved streets and auto registrations proliferating, TSR went into receivership. Service was cut to the bone; only the Main Street line had double-truck cars, the other lines had Birneys. In an effort to keep up with the city's explosive territorial growth, TSR was forced to crisscross the city with bus lines which competed with its own streetcars. The result was that neither mode made a profit.

In 1929 the assets of the company were sold for a paltry $233,334 to a group of investors which formed the United Service Co. In 1933 United Service took over the remaining city trackage of the Oklahoma Union Railway Co. (formerly the Oklahoma Union Traction). Except for the Sand Springs line, the city now had a unified transit network, but the Great Depression cut riding further and no financial remedy seemed possible.

On July 17, 1935, United Service went bankrupt. Its inventory sheet listed 16.9 miles of track (9.2 abandoned), 27 cars, 12 buses owned and 11 more being bought on time pay-

ments. Operations dragged on at a loss while company officials and the city tried to find a solution. Rail operations were down to a handful of single-truck Birneys, the relatively modern double-truckers having been sidelined as too expensive to operate.

Finally, on February 5, 1936, the company was sold at auction to National City Lines, a new national holding company being formed by the five Fitzgerald brothers, Roy, Edward, John, Ralph and Kent, of Minnesota, to buy up derelict local trolley lines as cheaply as possible and convert them to bus systems.

It was a new idea, and Tulsa was one of the first cities where it was tried. The Fitzgerald brothers had powerful backing from some of their major suppliers, such as Yellow Coach (later merged with General Motors) and the tire manufacturers. They were looking for cities with aging streetcars and life-expired tracks where the cost of fleet renewal with motor buses would be the cheapest solution. Of course, Yellow Coach would supply the buses, which would run on tires made by the same tire companies which invested in NCL.

NCL formed a local subsidiary, Tulsa City Lines, to take over operations effective the following day, February 6, 1936. Within hours TCL had enough buses on the streets to take over all operations, and the last city streetcar made its run up and down Main Street late that night.

Only the Sand Springs trolleys continued, still operated by the independent Sand Springs Railway. SS cars never entered the main part of downtown Tulsa, but loaded along Archer Street, north of the Frisco tracks. Nevertheless, the yellow SS cars continued to carry good passenger loads for another two decades.

Tulsa City Lines continued to operate from the old TSR barns on West Fifth, and gave Tulsa a citywide bus service until 1957, when the use of public transportation had declined to the point that NCL did not ask to renew the franchise. The city awarded a new franchise to MK&O Lines, which had a successful intercity bus operation centered in Oklahoma and now sought to enter the city transit field. MK&O furnished Tulsa with 75 new air-ride, 45-passenger General Motors coaches running on more frequent schedules than TCL had offered.

History eventually repeated itself as Tulsa, despite intensified growth in the 1960s and 1970s, found it could not sustain a privately owned transit system. As is universally the case, the city's bus system is now publicly owned (by the Metro Tulsa Transit Authority) and once again regaining viability in an era of skyrocketing gasoline prices and downtown rebirth.

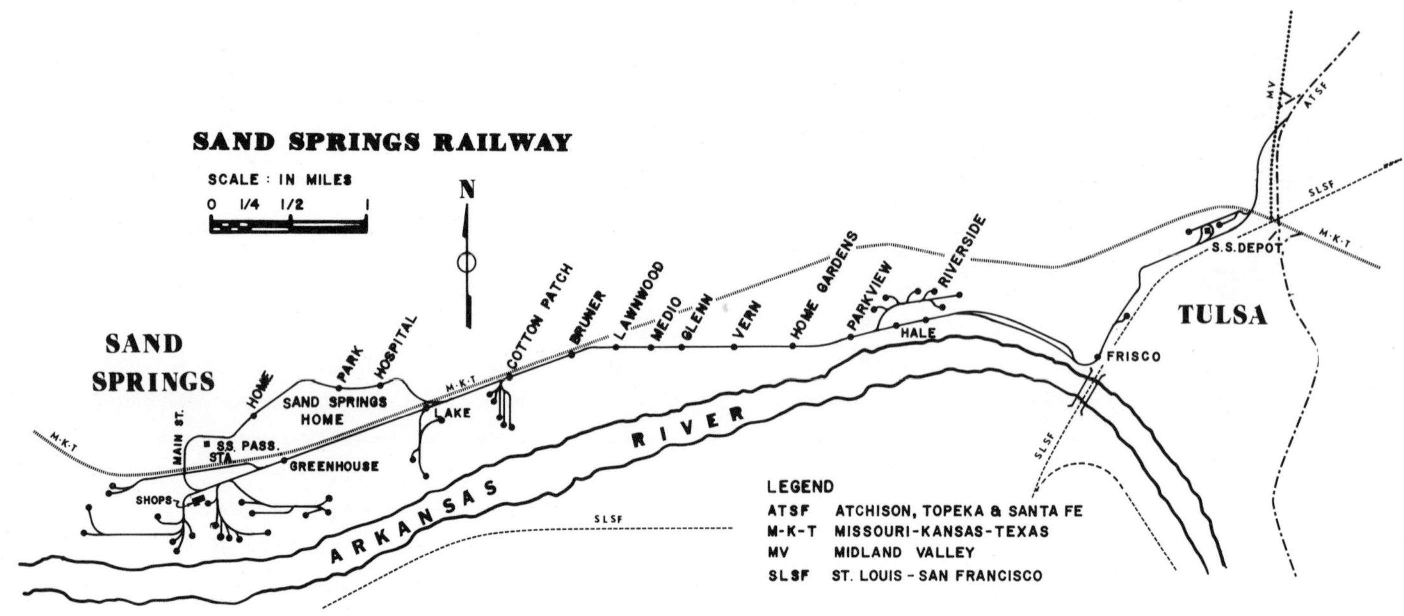

SAND SPRINGS RAILWAY
SCALE : IN MILES
0   1/4   1/2   1
N
SAND SPRINGS
HOME
PARK
HOSPITAL
SAND SPRINGS HOME
COTTON PATCH
BRUNER
LAWNWOOD
MEDIO
GLENN
VERN
HOME GARDENS
PARKVIEW
RIVERSIDE
HALE
MAIN ST.
S.S. PASS. STA.
GREENHOUSE
LAKE
M-K-T
SHOPS
ARKANSAS RIVER
SLSF
S.S. DEPOT
MV
ATSF
SLSF
M-K-T
FRISCO
SLSF
TULSA
LEGEND
ATSF   ATCHISON, TOPEKA & SANTA FE
M-K-T   MISSOURI-KANSAS-TEXAS
MV   MIDLAND VALLEY
SLSF   ST. LOUIS - SAN FRANCISCO

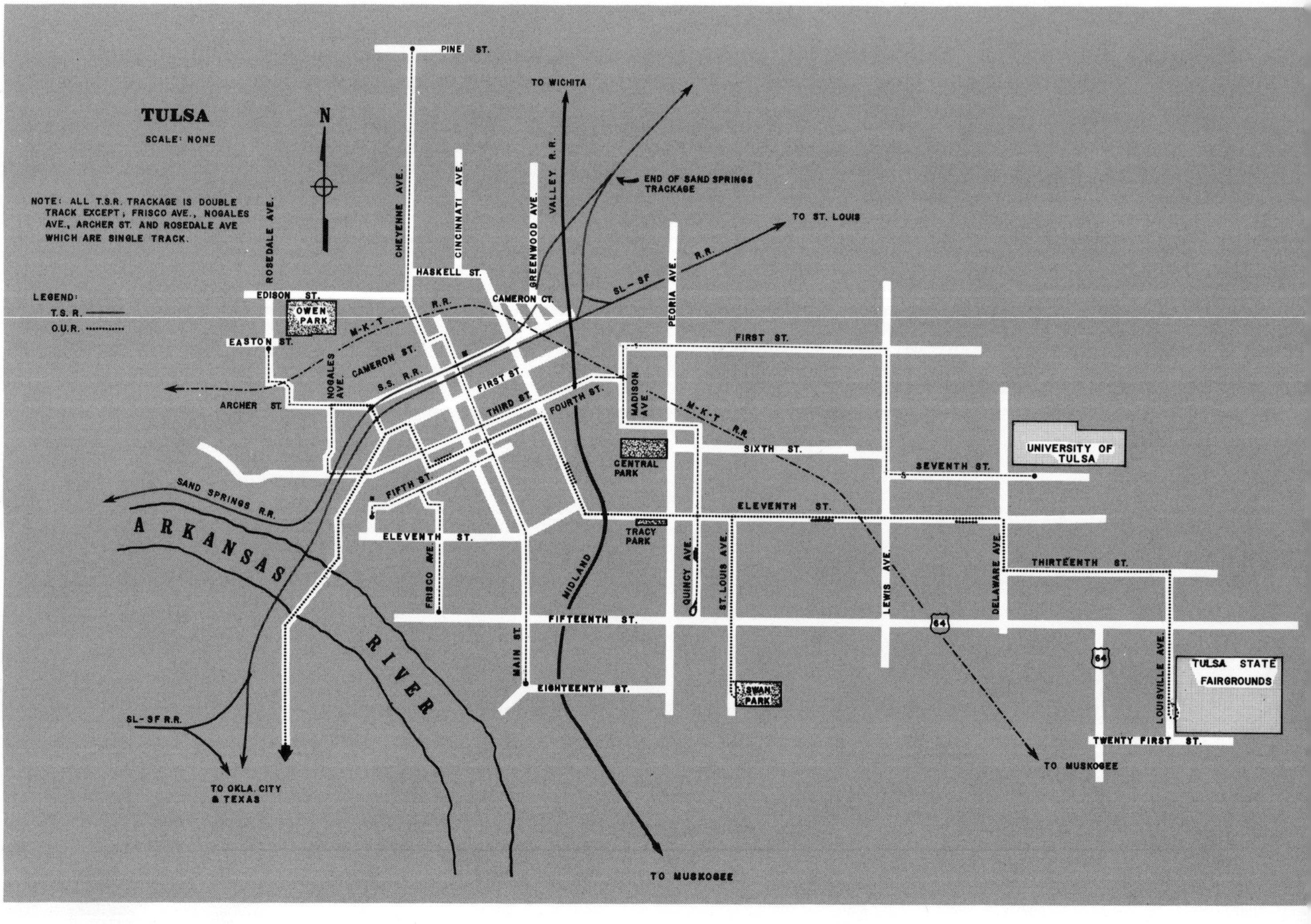

TULSA
SCALE: NONE
N
NOTE: ALL T.S.R. TRACKAGE IS DOUBLE
TRACK EXCEPT, FRISCO AVE., NOGALES
AVE., ARCHER ST. AND ROSEDALE AVE
WHICH ARE SINGLE TRACK.
LEGEND:
T.S.R.
O.U.R.
PINE ST.
TO WICHITA
END OF SAND SPRINGS TRACKAGE
TO ST. LOUIS
ROSEDALE AVE.
CHEYENNE AVE.
CINCINNATI AVE.
GREENWOOD AVE.
MIDLAND VALLEY R.R.
PEORIA AVE.
SL - SF R.R.
EDISON ST.
OWEN PARK
HASKELL ST.
CAMERON CT.
R.R.
FIRST ST.
EASTON ST.
M-K-T
NOGALES AVE.
CAMERON ST.
S.S. R.R.
FIRST ST.
ARCHER ST.
THIRD ST.
FOURTH ST.
MADISON AVE.
M-K-T R.R.
UNIVERSITY OF TULSA
CENTRAL PARK
SIXTH ST.
SEVENTH ST.
SAND SPRINGS R.R.
FIFTH ST.
ELEVENTH ST.
ELEVENTH ST.
TRACY PARK
QUINCY AVE.
ST. LOUIS AVE.
LEWIS AVE.
DELAWARE AVE.
THIRTEENTH ST.
ARKANSAS RIVER
FRISCO AVE.
MIDLAND
MAIN ST.
FIFTEENTH ST.
64
TULSA STATE FAIRGROUNDS
SWAN PARK
EIGHTEENTH ST.
64
LOUISVILLE AVE.
TWENTY FIRST ST.
TO MUSKOGEE
SL - SF R.R.
TO OKLA. CITY & TEXAS
TO MUSKOGEE

LEFT: When Tulsa Street Railway ordered a batch of single-truck Birney Safety Cars in 1919, it did not exactly insist on the last word in luxury. Slatted wooden seats were a fixture of this type of "economy model" streetcar. Management liked them; passengers didn't. This is car 340.
Jerry Moore Collection

BELOW: A quartet of these modern, arch-roof double-truck cars served the important Main Street line of TSR. Car 410 is pictured in front of the barn in the last days.
Magna Collection

TULSA STREET RAILWAY

FLEET NO.	BUILDER	ORDER	DATE	REMARKS
100,105	American	733A	7-15-07	ST 10 bench open. New.
200,205	American	738	8-13-07	ST closed city. New.
210,215,220	Barney&Smith		1909	ST closed city. New.
225,230,235,240	Barney&Smith		1910	ST closed city. New.
300,305?	McGuire-Cum		1913	DT closed city. Acq 1920s from Dayton Spfd & Xenia Sou RR 27,29
310,315,320, 325,330,335	American	1126	4-3-18	ST Birney. New.
340,345,350, 355,360,365	St Louis	1204	11-3-19	ST Birney. New.
400	Jones		1892	DT closed city. Acq 1909 Boston El Ry 1212. Orig. horsecar.
405,410,415,420 425,430,435, 440,445,450,455	American	1095	12-13-17	DT closed city. New.
	American	88	1894	DT closed city. Acq 5/1913 Phila Rapid Transit 514,518,525,537,539,569, 587; Orig. El. Tr. Co. 14,18,25,37,39,69,87.
(1 car)	Wason	103	1919	ST Birney. Acq Danbury & Bethel Pwr & Transp 45-53 series (CT).
(2 cars)	Wason	108G	1919	ST Birney. See above.
(4 cars)	Wason	108G	1920	ST Birney. See above.
(2 cars)	Wason	1150	1921	ST Birney. See above.

NOTE: 6 ST Birneys were acquired 5/1927 via Transit Equipment Co. and 3 ST Birneys in 4/1928 from the same source.

(4 cars)	American	1150	1-23-19	ST Birney. Acq 1928 from Peekskill Lighting & RR 30-35 (NY).
(2 cars)	Wason	108E	1920	ST Birney. See above.
?	Brill	12950	1903	ST trailers. Ex-Int. Traction Co., NY.

Work equipment included one ST, 2-motor sand car and one 4-motor DT work car.

ABOVE: On the loop at Sapulpa, interurban 101 takes some spot time prior to departure for Tulsa. It is November 1931, the company is already in bankruptcy, and passenger service would be ended within two years.
John B. Fink Collection

RIGHT: Early Tulsa Oklahoma Union Railway destination was Orcutt Park, now called Swan Lake. Car 17 lays over at the park about 1917. *Jerry Moore from Stephen D. Maguire*

13. TROLLEY POLES AND OIL RIGS

ALTHOUGH NOT the first electric railway to be built in Oklahoma, the Tulsa-Sapulpa Union Railway holds one distinction—it was the last electric railway to operate in the state and one of the few juice-powered short lines to survive into the 1960s anywhere in the U.S.

The beginnings of the line date to the incorporation in July of 1907 of the Sapulpa & Interurban Railway. The line was to be built from Sapulpa, not to Tulsa—which was at the time smaller than Sapulpa and not regarded as a very important place—but to the newly discovered oil fields at Glenn Pool and nearby Kiefer, a total of 10.86 miles.

Nineteen seven was a year of tumult for Oklahoma; on November 16 of that year President Theodore Roosevelt signed the statehood bill, making Oklahoma the 46th state in the Union. A Wall Street panic that same year depressed the construction of new interurban railways elsewhere, but the area around Sapulpa was booming and needed transportation.

The new line opened for service in March 1908; later that year the tracks reached the hamlet of Mounds, five miles further south. Initial rolling stock included a pair of single-truck closed passenger cars built by the American Car Co. of St. Louis; five more were added within a year built by the St. Louis Car Co.

Meanwhile, Tulsa, 12 miles north of Sapulpa, began to experience the rapid growth which eventually made it into Oklahoma's second city. In 1909 Tulsa already had one streetcar system, but it was deemed by some of the city's leaders to be inadequate and so a second enterprise was launched: the Oklahoma Union Traction Co. The OUT and the S&I were eventually to be merged and linked into one system.

In April 1909, a charter was granted to Albert A. Small, C.L. Holland, E.T. Tucker, G.C. Stebbins and S.A. Orcutt to form the OUT for the purpose of building a crosstown streetcar line between Owen Park on the west and Orcutt Lake on the east. Despite the opposition of the rival Tulsa Street Railway, the city of Tulsa issued a franchise to the Small group. TSR managed to force the issue to a public vote, but on July 27, 1909, the voters of Tulsa affirmed the new road's right to operate. One factor in the electorate's favorable decision was the promise of the OUT to build an interurban line to Sapulpa, which was still enjoying its oil boom.

The OUT opened its Orcutt Lake line (now called Swan Lake) on December 22, 1909, but completion of the other end of the line, to Owen Park, was delayed until 1911 due to a noisy dispute with the TSR over a franchise for West Third

Street. In 1910 the company announced signing of a construction contract for the Sapulpa interurban, but nothing further was heard about the project for some time.

In Sapulpa, the S&I built two local car lines, the Fife Place line which formed a large loop in the southern part of the city, and the Forest Park line which reached the Euchee Indian Mission in the eastern part of town. Despite a local prosperity borne of black gold, the Sapulpa & Interurban was bankrupt by 1912. It continued to operate, was reorganized for a time as the Sapulpa Electric Interurban Railway until it was merged with the Oklahoma Union Traction.

In 1917, the year the U.S. entered World War I, the combined properties became the Oklahoma Union Railway Co. This included the five miles of Tulsa local lines, the former S&I interurban and city lines, and a newly revived scheme to build a connecting link between Tulsa and Sapulpa.

Construction began in January 1917. Tulsa's population had climbed to 75,000 and it was undergoing a bigger version of Sapulpa's early oil boom. Sapulpa by this time was on the decline, although few realized it. Its 1917 population was estimated as 20,000.

The new Sapulpa interurban branched off from the OUR's local Owen Park line in downtown Tulsa, paralleled the Frisco Railroad and crossed the Arkansas River on the county highway bridge. The line then ran through the suburb of Red Fork, home of several oil refineries and tank farms.

Construction of the interurban was a bit above contemporary interurban standards. Deep cuts and heavy fills leveled the rolling terrain between Tulsa and Sapulpa and permitted completion of a line a mile and one-half shorter than the Frisco. Wooden trestles were avoided; all bridges were of concrete construction, eight of them of arched design still kept in good condition by company forces in the 1960s. This was said to be because the company feared fire from the heavy oil pollution in the creeks.

Gradients were kept within one percent and curvature within two degrees.

OUR construction forces had considerable difficulty with the numerous creeks and waterways encountered. This necessitated construction of more than the usual number of culverts and bridges; at one point the engineers had to change the course of Onion Creek to avoid three crossings within a few hundred feet. Grade crossings were avoided except near the two terminal cities.

It was decided to use the former S&I powerhouse in Sapulpa to provide most of the electric power; the rest was purchased from the Public Service Co. of Oklahoma. Some power also came from the Sand Springs plant of the Sand Springs Railway.

One obstacle which was conquered by the OUR in building its new line was peculiar to the "oil patch": the dense network of oil pipelines connecting the many pumping wells in the vicinity. The company had to pay to bury all of these lines beneath its tracks; even more unique was the fact that in several locations the OUR tracks had to carefully cross operating push rods connecting well pumps to their remote power sources.

The Sapulpa interurban was opened with a flourish in October 1918. The 13 miles of new line brought the company's combined system to 27.2 miles of single track.

To operate its new interurban and to rejuvenate its one Tulsa and two Sapulpa city routes, the OUR purchased 15 new cars in early 1918, including six combines for intercity service and nine single-truck Birney Safety Cars for the local lines. This was followed later in the year by an order for two double-truck Birneys, a longer version of the single-truck car, for service on the company's Fair Grounds extension in Tulsa.

OUR's gross revenue blossomed from $10,371 in August 1918, when it counted only the Tulsa local line, to $34,989.40 in July 1920 covering the Tulsa and Sapulpa locals, and the interurban lines.

By this time the company also had an express motor, making at least one round trip a day all the way from Tulsa to Keifer (passengers had to change cars in Sapulpa). Oil-well supply houses were frequent customers. Along company tracks also was located the Cosden Refinery, said at the time to be the second largest in the U.S., although Cosden used steam railroads for the most part for shipment of its products; the interurban's role as an important carload freight feeder was to come later.

The substantial-looking interurban combines received in 1918 from the American Car Co. and numbered 101-106 were each 56 feet long with a nine-foot baggage compartment, a smoking compartment and a general passenger section seating 50. They had Brill trucks and Westinghouse air brakes.

Hourly service was given between Tulsa and Sapulpa, the trip taking 45 minutes for the approximate 16-mile ride, downtown to downtown. By the mid-1920s the Tulsa city service consisted of through runs between Red Fork and the Fair Grounds, with every other car turning back at West Tulsa. Fifteen-minute service was given (30 minutes to Red Fork) and six cars were required, a mixture of single and double-truck Birneys.

In this period the company affiliated itself with three

ABOVE: Main and Dewey streets in downtown Sapulpa was a mighty busy place back in 1912 when two city cars of the Sapulpa & Interurban mix it up with a throng of citizens. The occasion was a civic celebration of Oklahoma Statehood Day.
Stephen D. Maguire Collection

RIGHT: Early halftone shows Sapulpa & Interurban railway car on the right-of-way near Kiefer, circa 1912. Note oil storage tank at left, and those pipes in foreground may have been power rods going to nearby oil wells. *Stephen D. Maguire Collection*

short-line steam railroads, the largest of which was the Oklahoma Southwestern. A network of other short lines was planned to cover parts of Eastern Oklahoma, but an increasing financial pinch snuffed out these plans.

Passenger receipts on the main line and on the branches south of Sapulpa were hit hard by the swing to private automobile driving in the 1920s, but some of the slack was taken up by a newly developed business of carload freight switching, particularly in the Tulsa area. Utilizing the OUR's Tulsa streetcar tracks as a terminal railroad brought problems, as veteran OUR motormen remembered in a 1957 *Tulsa Tribune* newspaper interview.

William Harrold, then a city bus driver, recalled pulling "hundreds of boxcars" across the city's principal downtown intersection—Fourth and Main—in the dead of night after the OUR secured a contract to interchange cars from the Katy Railroad to the electrified Sand Springs line.

The city of Tulsa agreed to the operation, so long as it was conducted after midnight when it would not interfere with automobile traffic.

"We used a big electric motorcar (OUR owned no locomotives at the time) and pulled one boxcar at a time. We couldn't pull more than that because of the sharp corners—

they weren't like railroad curves," recalled Harrold. He was talking about the regular streetcar curves at Fourth and Elgin, Fourth and Elwood and First and Elwood.

"As it was, we had to sort of drag each car around the corners and it would usually jump the tracks. We carried along a big 'frog' to get cars back on the rails." (A 'frog' is a metal device to guide the flanges of a car wheel back onto the rail.) Another ex-OUR employee, Oliver C. Spencer, recalled that the OUR borrowed a Sand Springs electric locomotive for this service, but the unit's end corners were too square and wouldn't permit the boxcars to negotiate the corners. The locomotive was soon returned to the Sand Springs line.

The Katy brought cars in from its Muskogee line to the OUR interchange on East 11th and Zunis Ave. on the Fair Grounds streetcar line. The cars would then be hauled through downtown to the Sand Springs interchange with the OUR at First and Guthrie. Some cars went instead to the Frisco interchange in West Tulsa.

"The company always put the crew with the longest service on the night transfer run," recalled Spencer. "It required exact skill to get the cars through town. We could move about 12 or 15 cars a night between the Katy tracks and the Sand Springs line terminal."

Flanked by crewmen on each platform, a pair of stylishly hatted ladies remain inside Sapulpa & Interurban car 3 while the photographer does his work, circa 1910.
Merle Ford Collection

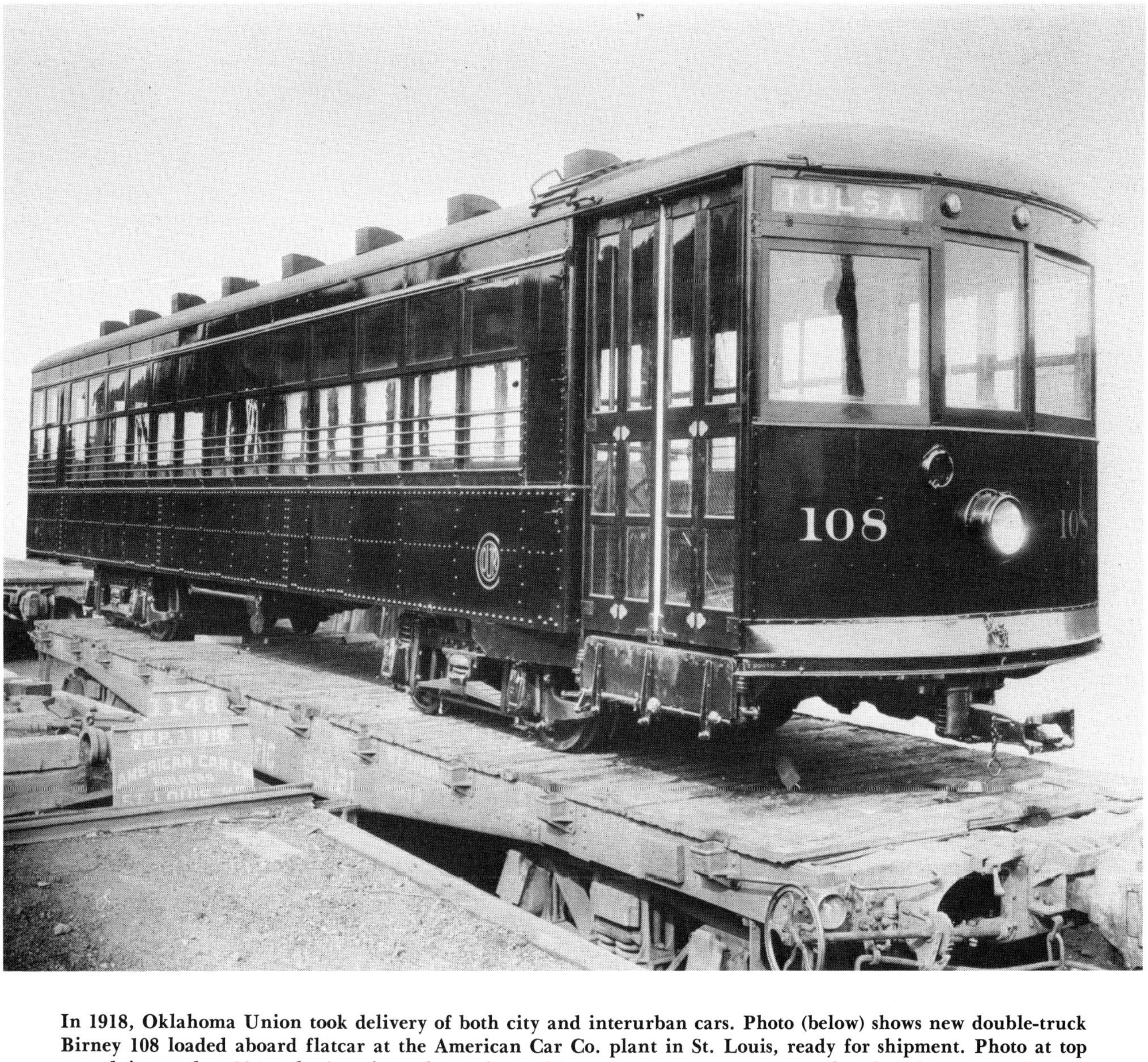

In 1918, Oklahoma Union took delivery of both city and interurban cars. Photo (below) shows new double-truck Birney 108 loaded aboard flatcar at the American Car Co. plant in St. Louis, ready for shipment. Photo at top records interurban 104 at the American plant prior to shipment. *Both: Edward Watson Collection*

Such heroic efforts to make a few extra dollars on freight interchange did not save the OUR. The original SI line south of Sapulpa, to Mounds, was abandoned in 1928. The OUR itself tumbled into bankruptcy a year later. All electric passenger service ended in 1933, with the Tulsa city line turned over to United Service Co., successor to the Tulsa Street Railway. Company-owned buses replaced interurban cars between Tulsa and Sapulpa.

In 1934 the company reorganized as the Sapulpa Union Railway, still offering electric freight service between Tulsa and Sapulpa. On the Tulsa end, trackage was cut back to West Tulsa, about four blocks south of the Arkansas River bridge and near the large Mid-Continent Petroleum Co. refinery. Connections were made here with the Frisco and the Midland Valley belt railway.

The company entered World War II with a rundown physical plant, but climbing revenues. The trackage had never been fully ballasted, and by this time the rails and ties were in poor shape, and some of the rotting wooden poles supporting the electric overhead were leaning at odd angles.

A final name change occurred in 1943, when the line became affiliated with its largest on-line shipper, the Liberty Glass Co. of Sapulpa. The new name was the Tulsa-Sapulpa Union Railway. Twice-daily electric freight service was the rule, with the main cargo silica sand, limestone and soda ash to the Liberty plant just north of Sapulpa.

Money was spent to upgrade the line. Back in 1939 the company had been able to pick up a pair of Cincinnati & Lake Erie freight motors, 202 and 203, at a sacrifice price. After the Sand Springs Railway converted to diesel propulsion in 1955, the TSU purchased two of its 50-ton electric locomotives, the 1002 and 1004.

Prior to this purchase, it had been widely predicted in both professional and railfan circles that the TSU electric operation would surely give way to diesel, but this did not happen until April 11, 1960.

In the late 1950s the line fought a prolonged and sometime acrimonious battle with the state highway department, which wanted to cross the TSU right-of-way with a new freeway. The highway department felt that total abandonment would be cheaper than building a single freeway overpass, and pointed out that the main line of the Frisco went right past the Liberty glass plant.

But the TSU held its ground, and the railway stayed in business, although it was shortened to the nearest mainline rail connection near the southern Tulsa limits. This left 10 miles of main line still in service between Tulsa and Sapulpa.

New paint job adorns Tulsa-Sapulpa box motor 203, circa 1940 just after its acquisition from the abandoned Cincinnati & Lake Erie interurban in Ohio. This unit and sister 202 performed yeoman service on the TSU until final retirement in 1955.
Texas ERA Collection

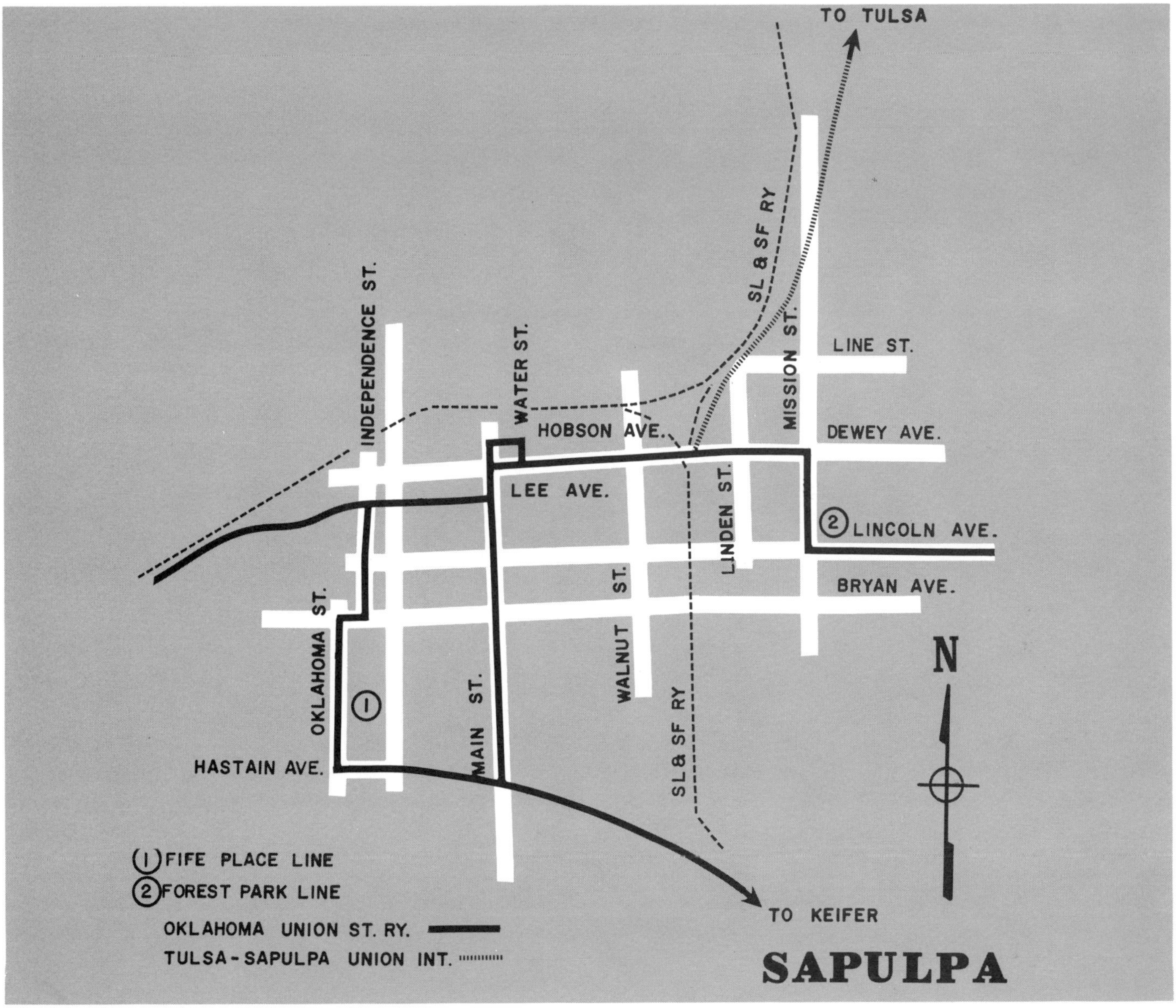

Many electric railways adopted patriotic paint jobs and slogans during World War II, and the Tulsa-Sapulpa was no exception. Here is ex-Cincinnati & Lake Erie box motor 203 switching at the Frisco interchange in West Tulsa during the war.
Texas ERA Collection

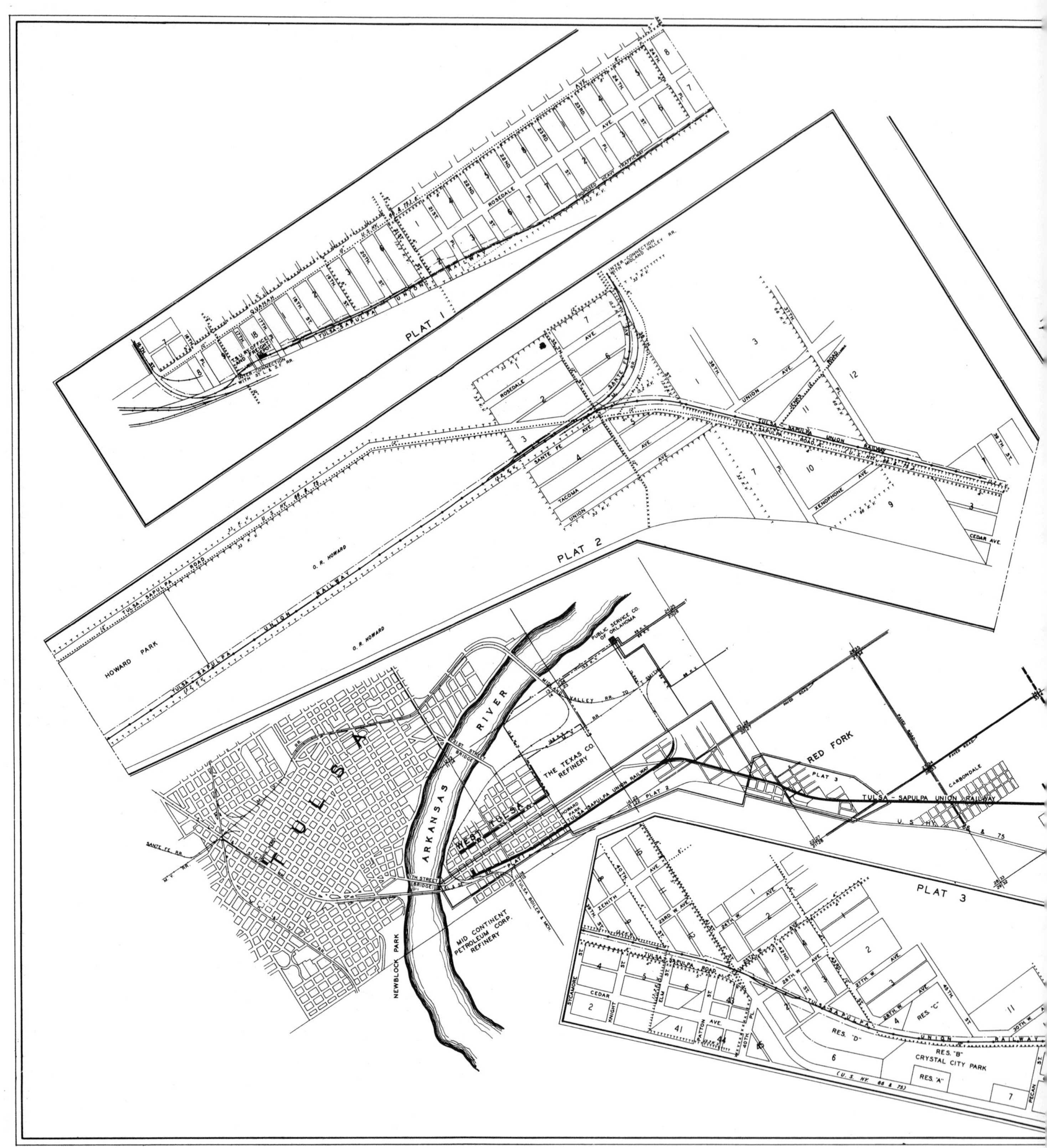

This map of the Tulsa-Sapulpa mainline of the TSU was issued by the company about 1950 and shows mainline railroad connections. In passenger days, the line continued across the 11th Street bridge into downtown Tulsa.   *TSU*

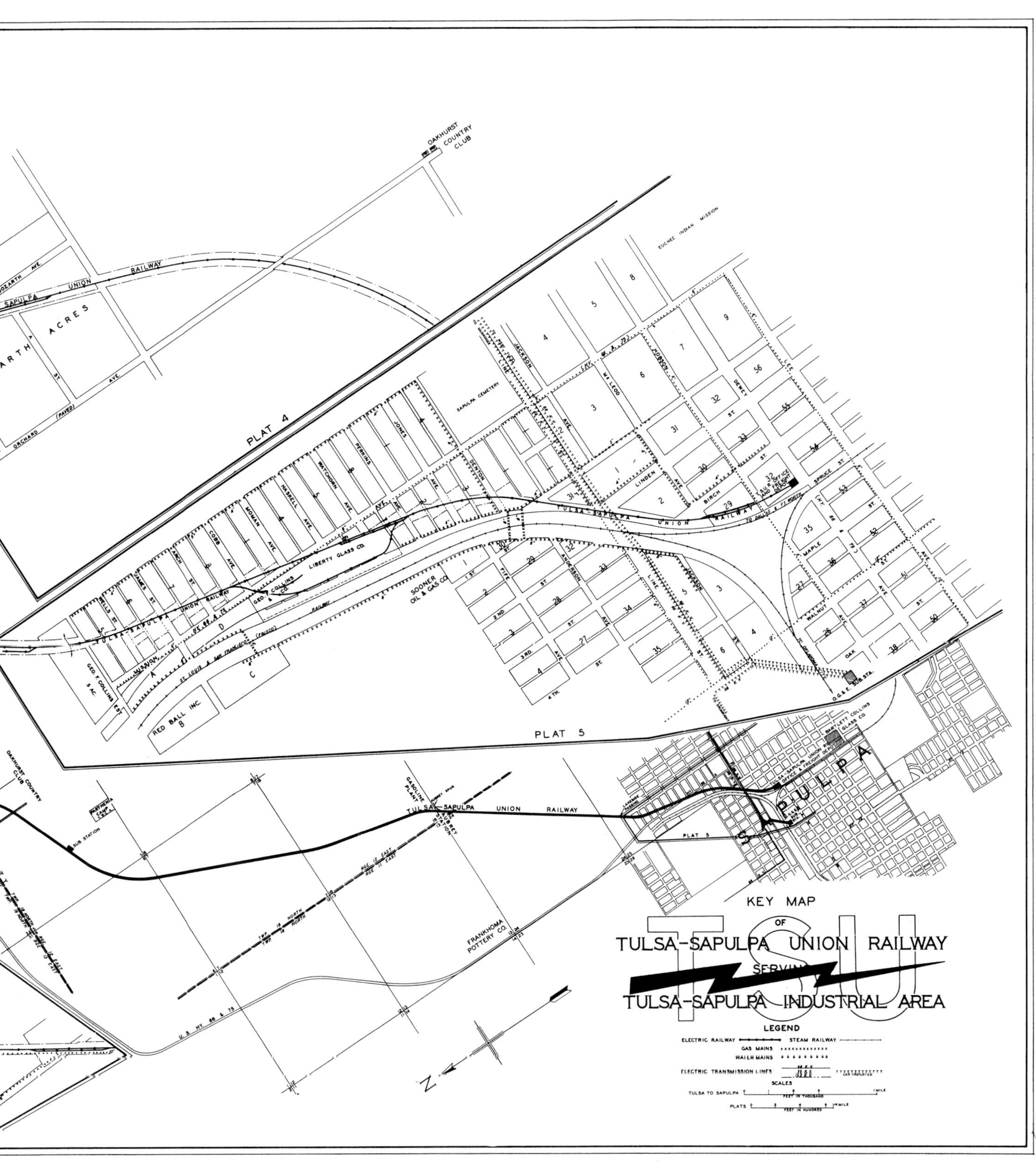
KEY MAP
OF
TULSA-SAPULPA UNION RAILWAY
SERVING
TULSA-SAPULPA INDUSTRIAL AREA
LEGEND
ELECTRIC RAILWAY   STEAM RAILWAY
GAS MAINS
WATER MAINS
ELECTRIC TRANSMISSION LINES
SCALES
TULSA TO SAPULPA   FEET IN THOUSAND   1 MILE
PLATS   FEET IN HUNDRED   1/4 MILE
PLAT 4
PLAT 5
SAPULPA
OAKHURST COUNTRY CLUB
EUCHEE INDIAN MISSION
TULSA-SAPULPA UNION RAILWAY
SAPULPA CEMETERY
LIBERTY GLASS CO.
SOONER OIL & GAS CO.
RED BALL INC.
FRANKHOMA POTTERY CO.
GASOLINE PLANT
U.S. HY 66 & 75

Box motor miscellany: Motors 202 and 203 were the maid-of-all-work on the freight-only Tulsa-Sapulpa Union for a decade and a half. Here is a quartet of photos taken out on the line about 1946; bottom photo, with billboards, is near TSU's West Tulsa terminal. *All: Texas ERA Collection*

Prime movers on the TSU after 1955 was a pair of Baldwin-Westinghouse center-cab juice locomotives purchased from neighboring Sand Springs Railway when the latter converted to diesel operation. Here they sit behind the Sapulpa shops in the early morning hours of May 17, 1959, awaiting the day's assignments.

Both: Fred W. Schneider III

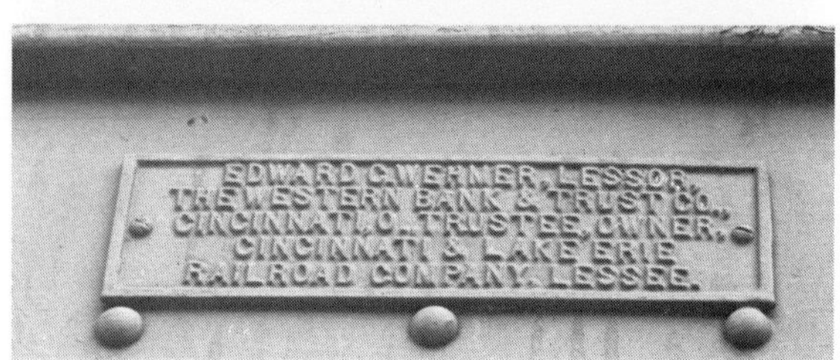

After the ball is over: Box motors 202 and 203 sat forlornly behind the barn at Sapulpa for years after their 1955 retirement. Here are closeups of the ravishes of time. (Top) Original Cincinnati & Lake Erie equipment trust plate was still in place. Photos were taken on May 17, 1959.

All: Fred W. Schneider III

TULSA-SAPULPA UNION RAILWAY

Sapulpa & Interurban Ry. Co. in 1911 had 8 passenger cars, 1 service car (2 DT 4 ST and 2 tlr); succeeded in 1916 by Sapulpa Electric Interurban Ry. The 2 double truck cars are believed to have been United RR of St Louis 586 and 752, acquired 1910. Car 586 was S&I 33. Also had a DT flatbed work motor, St Louis Car Order 835, 1909.

FLEET NO.	BUILDER	ORDER	DATE	REMARKS
1-2	American	799	1909	ST closed city. New.
3-6	St Louis	831	1909	ST closed city. New.
7	St Louis	833	1909	ST closed city. New.
14-16	American		1896	DT closed city. Acq 1909 from United RR of St Louis 951,947,952.
(1 car)	American		1894	DT closed city. Acq 1909 from United RR of St Louis 703.
30	?			DT flatbed work motor.
31-36	American	1112	3-30-18	ST Birney. New.
37-39	American	1113	2-22-18	ST Birney. New.
41-42	American	996	8-16-13	DT closed interurban. Ex-Nipissing Central Ry; Orig. E. St Louis, Columbia & Waterloo 30-31. May have been sold to Sand Springs Ry.
43	?			City car. Details unknown.
51-52	Brill	21316	5-20-21	ST Birney. Acq 9/1929 from Detroit St Ry 211, 226.
53-56	St Louis	1258	1921	ST Birney. Scq 9/1929 from Detroit St Ry 280,282,286,297.
101-102	?			
103-105	American	1114	8-10-18	DT interurban combine. New.
106	?			
107-108	American	1148	9-3-1918	DT Birney city. Sold 1934 Sand Springs Ry 69-70.
109-110	?			
111-113	?			DT interurban trailers.
200	?			DT locomotive. Scrapped 1940.
201	American	1115	7-9-1918	DT freight motor. New.
202-203	Cincinnati	3060	1929	DT freight motor. Acq 1939 Cincy & Lk Erie 648,641. Sold 1955 Borg Compressed Steel Co., Tulsa. 202 sold 1974 Seashore Trolley Museum.
1002	Bald-West	41893	2/1915	50t 400hp locomotive. Acq 1955, Sand Springs 1002.
1004	Bald-West	40537	6/1927	50t 400hp locomotive. Acq 1955, Sand Springs 1004.

NOTE: 1002 originally Cushing Traction Co 501. Both sold for scrap 1960.

TULSA-SAPULPA UNION DIESEL LOCOMOTIVES

FLEET NO.	TYPE	BUILDER	ORDER	DATE	REMARKS
2	B-B D/E	Davenpt	2363	3/1942	44t 360hp ex-Frisco 2. Sold Cherokee Nitrogen Co., Pryor OK; scr 1977.
101	B-B D/E	EMC	1075	5/1940	SW1, 600hp. Ex-Wabash 105, acq 1960
102	B-B D/E	GM-EMD	4730	4/1947	SW1, 600hp. Ex-Wabash 108, acq 1960
103	B-B D/E	EMC	1166	9/1940	SW1, 600hp. Ex-Ind Maint Svc (D), orig. EJ&E 229; acq. 12/1971.

NOTE: All of the SW1 locos ran for a time with their former numbers.

14. AN EARLY TRACTION CASUALTY

PERHAPS because it has come to be an important corporate headquarters city in the petroleum field, with an impressive skyline and an affluent population, Bartlesville has been called one of the most cosmopolitan little cities in the U.S. It boasted less than 30,000 residents in the 1970 census, but to the casual visitor the city might appear to be several times that size.

Explosive growth early in the century stimulated construction of a 10-mile city and interurban railway system linking Bartlesville and the suburbs of Tuxedo and Dewey. The line was comparatively short-lived, lasting only one day over 12 years. It was never profitable and, despite its acquisition by the Cities Service combine, which for a time made Bartlesville its oil company headquarters, it faltered badly after World War I and expired with the city fathers' only concern being that the tracks be promptly covered over.

The Bartlesville Interurban Co. was chartered in 1905 by John J. Curl, and was capitalized at $300,000. The company proposed to build a railway and operate its own power station. At the time Bartlesville was still part of the Indian Territory.

Construction began in 1907, with the tracks reaching Dewey, five miles northeast of Bartlesville, via Tuxedo, the National Zinc Co., the Bartlesville Zinc Co. and the Lanyon-Star Smelting Co., at that time the largest smelting combination in the world.

Revenue service started on July 14, 1908, on 7.8 miles of track. The power plant, costing $25,000, was completed in 1909 in Bartlesville. Initial rolling stock consisted of two 43-foot double-truck closed streetcars, purchased from the St. Louis Car Co.

Bartlesville's population of 4,215 in 1907 leaped to 9,000 in 1908, largely due to the extensive lead and zinc refining operations in the area. By 1909 the population had reached 12,000 and by 1915, 20,000. The new interurban reached most of the heavy employment centers.

In common with many small interurban companies in the early days, the Bartlesville Interurban Co. sold excess electricity to on-line towns (Bartlesville and Dewey were both customers) and this came to provide important revenue to the firm. On July 1, 1912, both the power and the interurban business were sold to the Harry L. Doherty Co. of New York, which eventually put the company into the Cities Service family.

On July 27, 1915, the company established an amusement park on the line between Bartlesville and Dewey, called Interurban Park. The park featured an open-air movie, rides, swings, a merry-go-round, a dance platform and pic-

Laying streetcar tracks in 1907 involved the use of a lot of animal and human power. Judging from the crowds, this was perhaps the ceremonial groundbreaking—although the ground was well broken before the ceremony.
Both: Griggs Studio Collection

nic grounds. The idea was to generate additional traffic for the streetcars; some 3,000 persons were on hand for the grand opening.

After its original purchase of cars, the company bought at least one additional interurban from the St. Louis Car Co. in 1911, and in the years 1913, 1914 and 1915 acquired three additional closed city cars.

As the city developed, Bartlesville Interurban planned new lines. On December 9, 1915, operation started on the "loop line" which left the main line at Fourth Street and Wyandotte Ave., on a 30-minute headway.

By 1916, trackage totaled 10.1 miles and eight cars were in service. Three years later the business was turned over to the Bartlesville Gas & Electric Co. and 11 cars were in service, the all-time high. There was talk of an extension 20 miles eastward to Nowata to connect with the Union Traction Co. of Kansas, but by that time railway losses were running as high as $500 per month.

The decision to abandon came soon after, and with approval from the Oklahoma Corporation Commission to cease operation, all cars returned to the carhouse on East Fourth Street on July 15, 1920, never to run again.

The power company continued in business, of course, and among its officers was Frank Phillips of the Phillips Petroleum Co. Phillips made Bartlesville its headquarters and largely accounts for the city's prosperity to this day.

Passing turnout was located near the end of the line in Dewey. Photo was taken in the very earliest days of service.
Griggs Studio Collection

TOP: Looking from Johnstone east on Third (now Frank Phillips Blvd.), view taken from top of building shows interurban just in from Dewey, circa 1909.   *Griggs Studio Collection*

BOTTOM: Two-man crew (with Guy Woodring at right) is ready to start for Dewey with car 1 after photographer is finished.   *Bartlesville Public Library*

TOP: Unpaved streets were a fact of Bartlesville life in 1910. View looks north on Johnstone Avenue.

Griggs Studio Collection

BOTTOM: The whole gang is out to celebrate as two Bartlesville Interurban cars pass at Third and Dewey streets, 1909. That overhood looks a little droopy.

Griggs Studio Collection

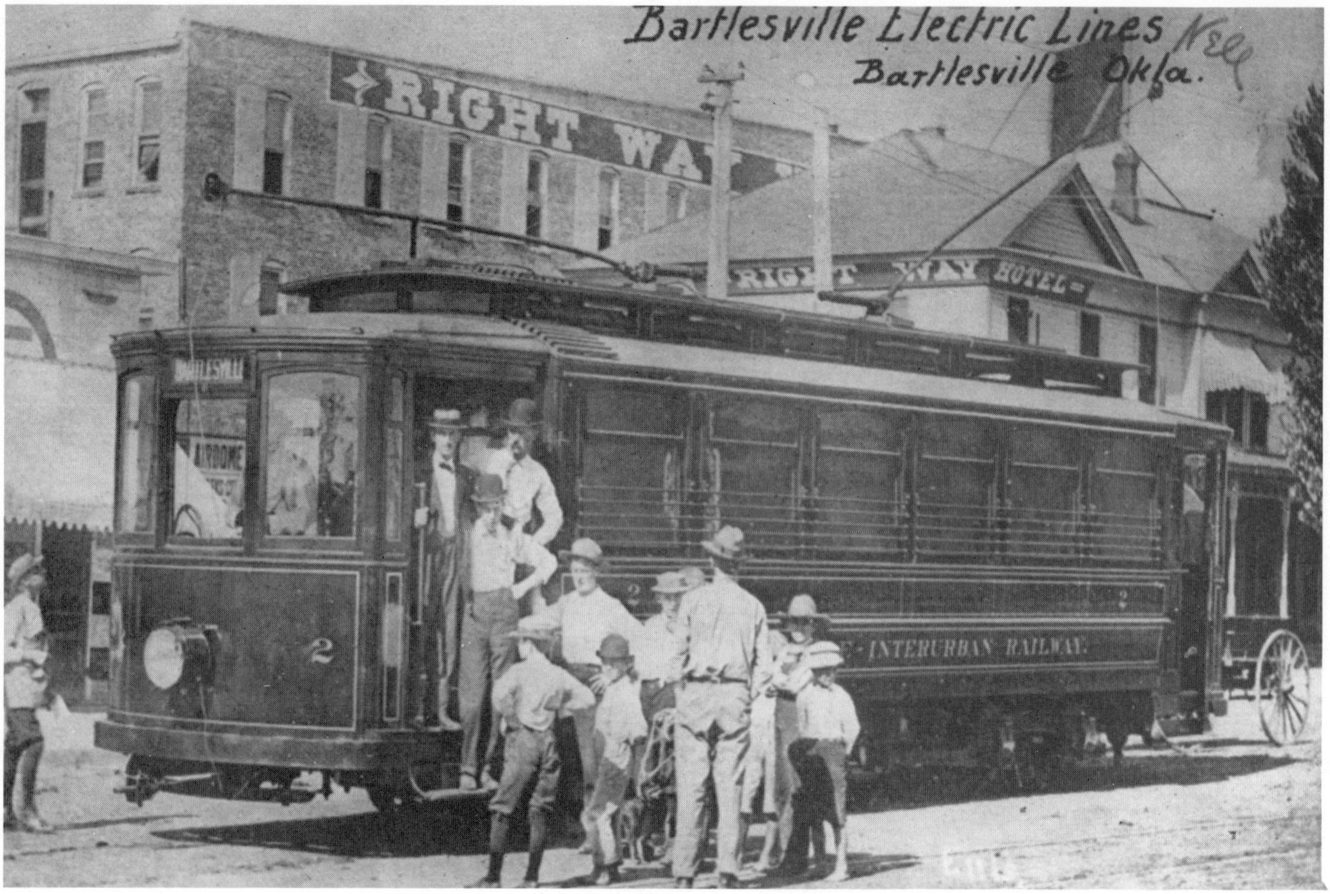

TOP: Here is car 2, playing host to an assemblage of Bartlesville residents, including small fry. Circa 1909.
Griggs Studio Collection

BOTTOM: Somewhere along the right-of-way between Bartlesville and Dewey we see car 4 taking a breather. With all windows wide open, passengers could enjoy a breezy ride to break the heat of a summer's day, circa 1912.
Bartlesville Public Library

Couple of streetcars get involved in the traffic tieup in front of the Daily Enterprise building, where this crowd is listening to a "broadcast" of the 1917 World Series. Before radio, newspapers used to post play-by-play reports of major sporting events via telegraph.
Griggs Studio Collection

BARTLESVILLE INTERURBAN COMPANY

FLEET NO.	BUILDER	ORDER	DATE	REMARKS
1-2	St Louis	789	4-20-08	DT closed city. New.
3	St Louis	?	?	DT closed city. New.
4	St Louis	815	12-30-08	DT interurban. New.
5	St Louis	893	1-19-11	DT closed city. New.
(2 cars)	St Louis	801	7-8-08	DT interurban. New.
101	St Louis	1010	7-7-13	ST closed city. New.
102	St Louis	1041	6-12-14	ST closed city. New.

One additional closed ST semiconvertible may have been acquired in 1915. In 8/1918 had 8 motor cars, 1 other, 10.1 miles of track.

What the Union Electric's dilapidated tracks have done to the brick streets of Independence, Kansas, is graphically demonstrated in this 1947 photo of car 74. On the other hand, the rest of the street didn't look to be in any great shape, either.
Gordon Zahorik

Nowata—Union Electric Railway

15. ONLY WALKING WAS CHEAPER

ONE OF OKLAHOMA's most remarkably durable electric interurbans was really a Kansas institution, but 22 of the Union Electric Railway Company's 77 miles of meandering trolley line were in Oklahoma, from Nowata to within three miles of Coffeyville, in the Jayhawk state.

The Union Electric was a fiscal marvel. From 1921 until its final abandonment on April 4, 1948, the Union was in financial hot water. It covered operating expense in only two of those 26 years, yet its management, believing always that next year would be better, continued to operate a small, battered fleet of trolleys over ever-deteriorating track. Fiercely loyal to their hometown trolley, the Union's patrons stuck it out to the end without complaint.

The system, cheaply built and poorly maintained, served no cities larger than 15,000 population yet it outlived by more than a decade some of the interurban giants of America. Until World War II the line was barely able to pay its bills. The opening of a munitions plant at Parsons and an air base at Independence, both in Kansas, and gasoline rationing, brought a brief period of prosperity to the company. Ironically, wartime shortages and constant passenger demand prevented the Union from rehabilitating its tracks and cars and by the mid-1940s the enterprise was once again sliding toward disaster.

Starting at Nowata, the line ran directly north for 25 miles to Coffeyville, Kan., then swung westward to begin a great arc, through Dearing and Jefferson to Independence, then back eastward again through Cherryvale and Dennis to Parsons, 52 miles from Coffeyville (compared to the 31-mile line of the Katy railroad between the two cities). Four hours were required for a through trip—but almost no one made a through trip. Local riding was the norm on the Union Electric.

Union Electric's predecessor, Union Traction Co., was chartered in 1907, uniting together the street railways of Coffeyville and Independence; the interurban was completed between them on July 14, 1907.

D.H. and Charles Siggins of Warren, Pennsylvania, were the promoters of the road. A large oil field had been discovered in Montgomery County, and Coffeyville's population jumped from 4,953 in 1900 to 12,306 in 1904; Independence zoomed from 6,218 to 11,456. Nearby cities grew as well. The Siggins brothers capitalized their new interurban at $500,000 with a bonded debt of $1 million. The two Pennsylvanians also built the Southwestern Interurban Railway between Winfield and Arkansas City, Kansas, just a few miles north of the Oklahoma line.

In a bizarre twist of fate, Charles Siggins became the line's first fatality when, on July 17, 1908, he was electrocuted near the Jefferson station of the interurban after he climbed on top of a car to do some repair work on the overhead trolley wire. It was about 1 A.M. and, thinking the power had been turned off, Siggins touched the wire. The electrical shock knocked him off the top of the car and he fell to the ground and was killed.

It was not long before neighboring Cherryvale, and Parsons, division point on the Katy Railroad, were bidding for Union Traction service; the extension to Cherryvale (10 miles northeast of Independence) was opened on March 1, 1910.

The Parsons extension was promised as early as 1911, the city residents of that city of 16,000 voted favorably on a bond issue to help with the cost of construction. Revenue service into Parsons commenced finally on December 21, 1912. The final extension, south from Coffeyville to Nowata, Oklahoma, was opened early in 1915.

Thirteen through trips a day were made from Coffeyville to Parsons, cut in 1917 to 12, while 11 runs a day were offered from Coffeyville to Nowata. In addition to the interurban trips, Union Traction operated local streetcar service in both Coffeyville and Independence, a service which endured to the very end in 1948 when streetcar service in towns of less than 20,000 was unique.

In 1917, talk was heard of an extension from Nowata southward to Tulsa which would have turned the Union Traction into a regional carrier, serving an important terminal city. Nowata is only 45 miles north of Tulsa. However the proposals emanated from an independent group of promoters, and Siggins was no longer interested in expansion. Nothing came of the proposal.

D.H. Siggins died on September 28, 1924, just as the company was experiencing mounting financial headaches due to the diversion of passengers to automobiles. The following year the company purchased a small fleet of double-truck Birney streetcars, which could be operated with a one-man crew. The old cars required both a motorman and a conductor.

The new cars were designed for duty as city streetcars, over rigid track set in concrete or asphalt. Few interurbans attempted to operate such an ultra-lightweight car on open track, especially track devoid of heavy ties and ballast. But Union Traction not only sent these cars clattering from one end of the 77 miles of interurban to the other, but kept them in operation for more than two decades. And then, when the Union was finally abandoned, managed to sell them to the Sand Springs Railway in Oklahoma for a further eight years of service!

As of February 1926, the company was running 14 through cars a day from Coffeyville to Parsons on roughly a 75-minute headway, while service on the Nowata line had been cut to seven trips a day. Lacking any meaningful extension to a large metropolitan center such as Tulsa, or even a small city such as Bartlesville, the Nowata extension was already proving unproductive.

Although interurban operations were making a thin profit, city line deficits in Coffeyville and Independence pulled the company into receivership in 1927. From then on, track and rolling stock maintenance was kept to a minimum. The Great Depression hit in 1930, and riding dwindled. The big Edgar Zinc Co. plant at Cherryvale closed in 1932, and more commuters were lost.

Under the receivership of John S. Layng, Sr., Union Traction's operations were tightened and its financial structure simplified. Layng had already been put in charge of the nearby Joplin & Pittsburg Railway, an electric interurban connecting Pittsburg, Kansas, with Joplin, Missouri. But

Rickety rails disappeared beneath the underbrush on the Union Electric, yet the company managed to scrape up a few dollars to repaint the front end of car 74, seen here crossing the Missouri Pacific mainline just north of Nowata, 1946. *Gordon E. Lloyd*

TOP: Coffeyville, Kansas, was the start of the run to Nowata as car 74 pulls out of the Union Electric depot at 7:45 A.M., September 1, 1946.

Gordon E. Lloyd

BOTTOM: Arriving at Nowata, car 74, operating as the 7:45 A.M. "train" from Coffeyville, gets set to enter the station wye. Elderly gentleman with suitcase is allowed to board now, a couple of minutes before the rest of the crowd.

Gordon E. Lloyd

whereas Layng had abandoned all passenger service on the J&P, he kept the Union Traction's yellow Birneys rolling. In 1937, the UT emerged from receivership as the Union Electric.

How did the Union do it, when other "country interurbans" were dying like flies? For one thing, the Union kept passenger fares at a penny a mile—only walking was cheaper. M.D. "Doc" Isely of Los Angeles, who wrote a book on another well-known Kansas institution, the Arkansas Valley Interurban (Interurbans Special 19, pub. 1956 and reissued 1977), had some thoughts on how the Union Electric managed to cling to viability:

"Let us compare the AVI with another Kansas line which was not so heavily constructed, so luxurious or so highly priced. The Union Traction served Coffeyville with 20,000 population, Independence with 13,000 and Parsons with 16,000 souls. It was 86 miles long (sic). The 59.6-mile AVI served the principal cities of Wichita (111,000), Newton (11,000) and Hutchinson (30,000). The population density is a fairly good indication of the potential business to be found—yet in 1937 the UT emerged from receivership

(with) lightweight, one-man equipment; mainline fares about one cent a mile . . . true, it had corrugated track and homemade special work, but people could afford to ride it. The AVI, with its stained glass, luxurious seating and expensive meter cabs for feeders (instead of three-for-a-dime streetcars) offered a ride of much higher quality but, at 3.6 cents a mile it was priced right out of the market. In later years the two-man AVI crew often outnumbered the passengers."

The AVI dropped passenger service in 1938, just as the Union Electric was getting a new lease on life. L.L. Francis, formerly the general manager, became president of the Union. Despite the line's popularity with its passengers, the cities of Coffeyville and Independence were becoming impatient with the company's deteriorating physical plant—especially the rickety tracks in city streets.

Coffeyville tried to rule the Union's cars off its streets, and Parsons forced amputation of the traction's downtown loop in return for a franchise extension. The Independence Chamber of Commerce urged the company to build a bypass; the UE did propose a $125,000 belt line but couldn't

Economy of one-cent-a-mile fares was stressed back in September of 1938 as Union Electric car 72 trundles down the main street of Nowata. No other form of public transport was cheaper and so, despite the rough ride, UER got its share of business.
Charles Smallwood Collection

afford to build it. Only the entry of the U.S. into World War II forced the cities to reconsider their opposition to city trackage, and the UE entered the hostilities with a healthy upswing in traffic.

By 1945, the UE's physical plant was a wreck and management proposed to eliminate passenger service and convert freight hauling to diesel propulsion. The Independence belt line proposal was revived, and Francis thought the line could prosper as a freight carrier, with passengers handled in buses.

But UE's bondholders—mostly descendants of the original investors—were fuming at the company's inability to pay dividends and felt that liquidation was the only course. Salvaging the company's assets would at least bring them

something. The argument raged on for two years, then final abandonment was the course decided upon.

Amazingly, the company was still running 11 cars a day north of Coffeyville, seven south to Nowata. On June 4, 1947, a bus was substituted for one of the through cars. In the following months, other schedules were motorized, and the last passenger car ran on July 17. Within a month, the five double-truck Birneys had been sold to the Sand Springs Railway and loaded on railroad cars for shipment to the Sooner State.

Freight operation limped along for a few months, with operations abandoned in piecemeal fashion, but by the following June the Union Electric had joined the vast majority of its rural interurban brethren in permanent limbo.

Kansas Highway 166 doubled as the mainline of the Union Electric out of Independence, as box motor 84 tows a single boxcar out of town in solitary splendor. Such short revenue trains hardly helped to keep the line open and, in fact, the UER was abandoned one year after this 1947 photo was taken.   *Gordon Zahorik*

ABOVE: Wabash gondola car is towed out of the Union Electric shops at Independence, Kansas, by UER locomotive 603. Carload freight brought much-needed revenue in good times and bad.
Gordon Zahorik

RIGHT: Battered but unbowed, Union Electric Birney 17 rests at end of Myrtle St. line in Independence early in 1945, while motorman "walks" the trolley pole around for the return trip to the Santa Fe Depot. ***Tom Langan Photo from C.J. DeVilbiss***

UNION ELECTRIC COMPANY

FLEET NO.	BUILDER	ORDER	DATE	REMARKS
15	American	834	11-27-09	ST closed city. New.
16	American	785	11-7-08	St closed city. New.
17?	Danville	?	1909	St closed city. New.
18	American	826	9-16-09	ST closed city. New.
25	American	1034	2-13-15	DT interurban combine. Rblt to freight motor, re# 64.
15-19 (2d)	Osgd Bradley	6750	1922	ST Birney. Acq. 1925 from United Elec Ry (RI) 1681,1689,1690,1692,1693.
21-28	(see note)			ST Birney.

NOTE: Origins of cars 21-28 are uncertain, but the following are known:

(3 cars)	Brill	21021	4/1920	Acq. 1925 from United Ry & Elec (Baltimore) 4025-4027.
(1 car)	St Louis	1254	6/1921	Acq. 1925 from Ark Valley Int (Wichita) 100; orig. blt on StL order 1081, 1-4-16 as Bosenberry 400, a very early lwt. demonstrator

33	American	897	4-13-11	ST closed city. New.
34	American	923	1-25-12	ST closed city. New.
35	American	925	1-26-12	ST closed city. New.
36	American	923	1-25-12	ST closed city. New.
38	St Louis	931	4-20-12	DT interurban express motor. New.
40,42,44	St Louis	930	4-20-12	DT interurban coach. New. Sold 1925 Sand Springs Ry 26,28,30.
50?	American	762	1908	DT utility car. New.
60	St Louis	1062	1915	DT freight motor. New.
62	St Louis	1121	11-18-16	DT freight motor. New.
64	American	1034	2-23-15	DT freight motor. Ex-combine 35.
80	Bald.-West.	45659	5/1917	50t, 960hp elec locomotive.
82	Bald.-West.	41054	12/1913	50t, 960hp elec locomotive.

NOTE: Both locos acq. 4/1933 from Youngstown & Ohio River Ry 5,3; sold 1948 to Mason City & Clear Lake 52-53 then to Iowa Terminal 60-61, 1961.

84	?	?	?	Locomotive.
6	?	?	?	Line car.
603	Okla Ry shops	–	1929	72t, 400hp elec locomotive
604	Okla Ry shops	–	1929	72t, 400hp elec locomotive

NOTE: Both locos acq. 1946 from Oklahoma Ry. (Okla City) 603-604. Sold 1948 Cedar Rapids & Iowa City 72-73 then resold 1954 Chicago, Aurora & Elgin 4004-4005.

70-75	American	1395	5-18-25	DT Lwt interurban. Sold 1947 Sand Springs Ry 76, 71-75. 46 seats.

TOP: Lone passenger prepares to board Northeast Oklahoma car 34 at Picher, Oklahoma, on May 6, 1934. Car is bound for Century, the end of the "fishhook."   *Robert V. Mehlenbeck*

BOTTOM: Miami was proud of its beautifully landscaped interurban turnaround loop, kept up at NEO expense. Car was typical of NEO's early heavy passenger equipment.   *Stephen D. Maguire Collection*

16. A FISHHOOK IN THE MINERAL BELT

TUCKED into the extreme northeast corner of the Sooner State was the Northeast Oklahoma Railroad, one of three connecting interurbans centering on Joplin, Missouri, and serving the Missouri-Kansas-Oklahoma tri-state mineral belt. As a freight carrier, the NEO outlasted its two partners by a very long span and, in fact, still exists as a branch of the St. Louis-San Francisco Railway.

The NEO traces its beginning back to 1908 as a steam short-line railroad, but it was not electrified until 1921, very late for a "new" interurban to start operations in the U.S. It was certainly the last new system to be launched in Oklahoma, and owed its beginnings and its preservation to the area's extensive lead and zinc mines.

The Oklahoma, Kansas & Missouri Inter-Urban Railway Co. was incorporated September 26, 1908, at Miami, county seat of Ottawa County and a small city of some 6,000 people. By early 1909 the company was operating about five miles of non-electrified track in the Miami area, with 15 additional miles projected in Oklahoma and to Baxter Springs, Kansas. Capitalization was set at $200,000.

The original rolling stock included a steam engine, two passenger coaches and two gasoline-electric railcars. Offices and repair shops were in Miami. Only the five miles from Miami to Commerce were completed until 1917, when the road was pushed northeast to Picher, near the Oklahoma-Kansas line, and doubling back south to Century, originally called Douthat. This 12-mile stretch resembled an upside-down fishhook, and it was eventually to prove to be the lifeblood of the line's passenger traffic.

In the 1916-1917 period numerous spur lines were extended to the lead and zinc mines in Ottawa County for shipment of minerals to smelters in Oklahoma, Kansas and Missouri. One short stretch of track pushed into Kansas a quarter of a mile to the Blue Mound Mine.

Passenger service in this period consisted of hourly self-propelled cars. The OKM had three 75-foot-long General Electric gas cars which it had obtained second-hand from an Illinois road and a daily steam-hauled mixed passenger and freight train.

On April 5, 1917, the OK&M dropped the word "Inter Urban" from its title and became simply the Oklahoma, Kansas & Missouri Railway.

After the end of World War I, the OK&M was doing well financially. The whole area it operated in was flat as a table and only a decade previously had consisted primarily of Indian farmland. About 1907, lead and zinc deposits were discovered around Commerce. Both the St. Louis-San Francisco (Frisco) and the Missouri, Oklahoma & Gulf (later the Kansas, Oklahoma & Gulf) mainline railroads ran nearby, but the OK&M was quickly organized to act as a mineral feeder line.

The onset of the Great War in 1916 and America's in-

Newly completed electric line of Northeast Oklahoma Railway on downtown Miami's Main Street, 1921.
Electric Railway Journal

Typical mine served by the NEO was at Picher. Photo circa 1921. *Electric Railway Journal*

volvement a year later accelerated the demand for lead and zinc and new mines were opened almost weekly; by the close of the war in 1918 some 280 mines were in operation in the area. It was a miniature replay of the early Colorado mining booms at Leadville and Cripple Creek.

Interestingly, practically all of the mines were located on land whose mineral rights had been leased from the original Indian owners, and it was said that some of the Indians enjoyed monthly incomes of $20,000 to $50,000 in royalties during the war years. Briefly, these tribesmen enjoyed wealth comparable to their cousins in the Osage and Creek Nation oil fields a few miles to the west.

Predictably, the close of the war led to a temporary slump in mining activity, but the railroad was just on the eve of big development. Rumors of electrification were rife, and on November 1, 1919, the Northeast Oklahoma Traction Co. was formed by a group headed by J.F. Robinson, who was president both of NEO and the Commerce Mining & Oil Co., the largest operator in the Miami field. The "traction" part of the company's name lasted only until December 16, 16 days after the new group took over the railroad. The final name of the firm became the Northeast Oklahoma Railroad Co.

By this time, Miami's population had risen to 8,000; Picher had 10,000 and Commerce, 7,500. A large percentage of the population was employed in the mines. Treece, Kansas, with a population of 3,000, was just beyond the end of the line.

The NEO was not alone in serving the needs of the area's mines. The Miami Mineral Belt Railroad penetrated the northern part of the NEO's territory and had a shorter connection with the Frisco at nearby Quapaw, Oklahoma. But the MMB was never electrified and there was business enough for both roads.

The new management quickly set about to rehabilitate

the line. Plans for electrification were confirmed, and the trackage upgraded. The new standard was 70-lb. rail on red and white oak ties, some of which were treated; chat ballast was used, that material being a plentiful byproduct of the mines.

By mid-1920 catenary-type overhead was being strung. Two substations were planned, but equipment delays forced operations to begin on December 20 with just the Picher

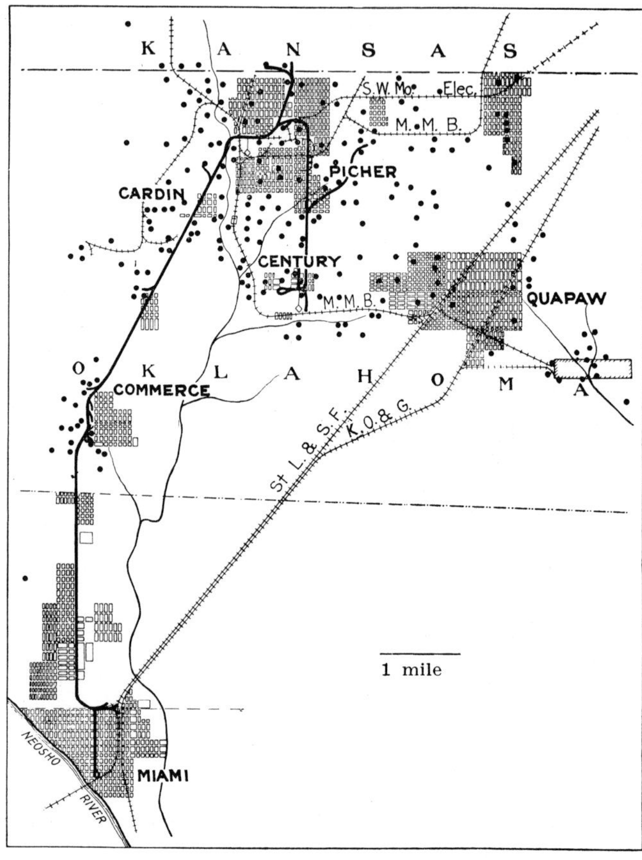

Map of the NEO, 1921, prior to extensions in Kansas.
Electric Railway Journal

facility operating, the substation equipment purchased used from the Cincinnati & Columbus Railway. The Commerce substation began operations later.

Likewise, the company was unable to secure new rolling stock in time to open electric operations, so it purchased a pair of interurban combine cars from the Nashville-Gallatin Interurban in Tennessee. Four smaller Jewett cars from the Cincinnati & Columbus followed in a few months.

By the early Fall of 1921, the entire 12-mile line was electrically operated, with mixed electric and steam freight operations retained. The General Electric gas-electric cars were sold to the Luce Electric in Minnesota, and the steam passenger coaches were retired.

In 1920, the NEO's gross passenger revenue totaled $81,172.87 while freight revenue was $189,867.55, giving an indication of the relative importance of the two types of business even that early. It was not long before the gap between freight and passenger revenues widened dramatically.

The Robinson management talked of an extension to Ponca City, Oklahoma, 140 miles to the west, but as it turned out the NEO struck out in an entirely different direction, and for different reasons.

Construction started northward in 1922, reaching Westville, Kansas, three miles from Picher, in that year and by early 1923, Columbus, Kansas, another nine miles. Before the severe recession of 1921 knocked wages back, motormen, conductors and mechanics on the NEO were making 62 cents an hour while brakemen drew 48 cents and trackmen 32 cents.

Four more used passenger cars were acquired in 1922-1923 and by the middle of October 1923 an hourly passenger schedule was in effect between Miami and Columbus. Overall, 66 daily passenger runs were operated. The line's extension to Columbus had been vigorously opposed by its territorial rival, the Joplin & Pittsburg, but once it was in operation it was possible to change cars in Columbus and ride all the way from Miami to Pittsburg, Kansas, by trolley. What the NEO was really after, though, was access to the many mines along the way, especially in the vicinity of Treece, Kansas. An additional benefit of the extension was a second direct connection with the Frisco Railway at Columbus.

In 1923 the NEO trackage totaled 25 miles of main line with an additional 20 miles in branches. And the line's

Merry Christmas was wished by NEO to all of its passengers and shippers each year in a parade which included this flatcar float.
Stephen D. Maguire Collection

owners had become a unit of the Eagle-Picher Mining & Smelting Co.

Most of the NEO's passenger business was concentrated on the original "fishhook" line, serving miners commuting to and from their pits. Half-hourly service was offered on this segment, hourly beyond. The Miami-Picher fare was 25 cents. Rolling stock included 14 electric passenger cars, all operated with two-man crews, one passenger trailer, 82 boxcars, 62 mineral cars, two electric and two steam locomotives.

Despite its mineral belt location, the NEO was something of a "spick-and-span" railroad. Management was especially proud of its Miami shops at the north edge of the city and its company offices in the downtown section of the city, whose population had settled down to about 7,000. Concrete, instead of wooden, poles were used in Miami to support the overhead wires, and a lavishly landscaped turnaround loop for passenger cars was maintained south of the Miami business district.

Power was purchased from the huge Riverton, Kansas, plant of the Empire District Electric Co., headquartered in Joplin, Mo.

Through rides to that Missouri city, the largest in the immediate territory, were available by taking the NEO cars to Picher where direct connection was made to the Southwest Missouri Electric Railway. This came about in 1918 when the SWM purchased and electrified steam road trackage from Baxter Springs, Kan., to Picher.

(In fact, it was possible to make a triangle trip with Picher, Pittsburg, and Joplin as the three corner points by using the cars of all three railroads, though the trip would have taken several hours.)

Passenger service retrenchments began in 1926, when the NEO slashed service on the Columbus line from hourly to two-hourly. Nevertheless, in that year the line carried $117,745.39 worth of passenger fares, 44 percent more than in 1920; gross freight revenue had mounted to $438,909.87, more than double the 1920 figure.

Heavy power for long freight trains was provided by this NEO electric locomotive.
Stephen D. Maguire Collection

In 1930 the Joplin & Pittsburg broke the passenger triangle by discontinuing interurban cars on the Columbus line. Later that year, J.A. Fenimore, owner of the reorganized J-P line, decided to sell almost the entire branch to the NEO, a 25-mile portion south of Cherokee, Kansas, for $100,000.

In the transaction NEO gained the five-mile Scammon-West Mineral branch as well, and its valuable connection with the Missouri Pacific at Carona for shipment of lead and zinc to the huge smelter in Collinsville, Ill., directly reached by the MP.

Now the NEO was a 77-mile railroad, with 50 of those miles in Kansas. The line's 1930 worth was reckoned at $1.5 million. This was sufficient to keep 170 employes (100 of whom lived in Miami) at work.

Suddenly, too, the NEO found itself to be a major Kansas interurban. In 1931 the NEO took in $20,469 in gross passenger revenue and $181,519 in freight revenue on its Kansas trackage, not overwhelming in its own overall totals but good enough to make it the second-largest interurban freight hauler in the Jayhawk state, after Wichita's Arkansas Valley Interurban.

In 1933 the portion of the West Mineral line west of the Corona MP connection was abandoned, and in September of that year all passenger service in Kansas north of Scammon ceased. The rest of the Kansas passenger service, north of Picher, Okla., was lopped off in 1934 although to improve passenger service on the original "fishhook" line, the NEO purchased a pair of lightweight Cincinnati "Curved Side" cars from Northampton Transit.

However, on January 16, 1936, most "fishhook" commuter runs were taken over by buses. Some of the remaining interurbans were kept in service to connect with Southwest Missouri's Joplin cars at Picher but this through service was cut the following year when the SWM abandoned passenger service east of Galena, Kansas. By 1939 all SWM passenger runs ceased and the NEO expanded again by purchasing that part of the SWM between Picher and Baxter Springs, Kansas, seven miles, in order to continue freight service to several mines.

This latest expansion prompted NEO management to take a good look at the possibility of dieselization of all motive power; in October of that year the first diesel, an 80-ton, 500-hp unit, was put in service. A few mainline railroads were already using diesel-electric locomotives as switchers in place of steam, and the NEO was one of the first of the short-line roads to convert.

In turn, the NEO decided to eliminate the last electric car commuter runs on the Miami-Picher line; in December 1939, car 34, one of the Cincinnati lightweights, made the last run. The company continued to operate buses.

A second diesel locomotive was acquired in December 1939 and a third in June 1940, when the electricity was turned off for the last time. The NEO now employed 133 people and had a yearly payroll of $175,000. World War II brought another upswing in business, and the need for more diesels. The company continued to operate its diesel freight and passenger buses into the 1950s, making such improvements as radio train dispatching and upgrading track, though much of the Kansas division was progressively abandoned.

The NEO, nicknamed the "Ore Line," survived under its own name until 1967, when the still-operating Baxter Springs-Picher-Miami portion was absorbed into the Frisco.

Extra-long juice locomotive 402 is shown parked next to one of the NEO's lightweight Cincinnati curved-side passenger cars, circa 1937. *Texas ERA Collection*

Steam and diesel propulsion were long used on the NEO, even during the electric days. (Top) This 2-8-0 steam locomotive served the NEO's main and non-electrified spur lines for many years. After the end of all electric operation, diesels took over completely. (Middle) Center-cab 257 is shown at Miami, 1950, (bottom) while pair of road-switchers hauls a freight train near Commerce, 1959. Note continued use of "Ore Line" slogan.
All: Stephen D. Maguire Collection

TIME ✦ TABLE

Northeast Oklahoma Railroad

CARS LEAVE MIAMI		CARS LEAVE COMMERCE			CARS LEAVE CARDIN			CARS LEAVE PICHER		CARS LEAVE CENTURY
FOR Commerce Cardin Picher	FOR Century	FOR Miami	FOR Cardin Picher	FOR Century	FOR Commerce Miami	FOR Picher	FOR Century	FOR Cardin Commerce Miami	FOR Century	FOR Picher Cardin Commerce Miami
* 6.00 am	* 6.00 am	* 6.48 am	* 6.10 am	* 6.10 am	* 6.43 am	* 6.15 am	* 6.15 am	* 6.37 am	* 6.20 am	* 6.30 am
7.00 am	7.00 am	7.48 am	7.10 am	7.10 am	7.43 am	7.15 am	7.15 am	7.37 am	7.20 am	7.30 am
8.00 am	9.00 am	8.48 am	8.10 am	9.10 am	8.43 am	8.15 am	9.15 am	8.37 am	9.20 am	9.30 am
9.00 am	11 00 am	9.48 am	9.10 am	11.10 am	9.43 am	9.15 am	11.15 am	9.37 am	11.20 am	11.30 am
10.00 am	1.00 pm	10.48 am	10.10 am	1.10 pm	10.43 am	10.15 am	1.15 pm	10.37 am	1.20 pm	1.30 pm
11.00 am	3.00 pm	11.48 am	11.10 am	3.10 pm	11.43 am	11.15 am	3.15 pm	11.37 am	3.20 pm	3.30 pm
12.01 pm	5.00 pm	12.48 pm	12.10 pm	5.10 pm	12.43 pm	12.15 pm	5.15 pm	12.37 pm	5.20 pm	5.30 pm
1.00 pm	7.00 pm	1.48 pm	1.10 pm	7.10 pm	1.43 pm	1.15 pm	7.15 pm	1.37 pm	7.20 pm	7.30 pm
2.00 pm	9.00 pm	2.48 pm	2.10 pm	9.10 pm	2.43 pm	2.15 pm	9.15 pm	2.37 pm	9.20 pm	9.30 pm
3.00 pm		3.48 pm	3.10 pm		3.43 pm	3.15 pm		3.37 pm		
4.00 pm	†11.00 pm	4.48 pm	4.10 pm	†11.10 pm	4.43 pm	4.15 pm	†11.15 pm	4.37 pm	†11.20 pm	
5.00 pm		5.48 pm	5.10 pm		5.43 pm	5.15 pm		5.37 pm		
6.00 pm		6.48 pm	6.10 pm		6.43 pm	6.15 pm		6.37 pm		
7.00 pm		7.48 pm	7.10 pm		7.43 pm	7.15 pm		7.37 pm		
8.00 pm		8.48 pm	8.10 pm		8.43 pm	8.15 pm		8.37 pm		
9.00 pm		9.48 pm	9.10 pm		9.43 pm	9.15 pm		9.37 pm		
†10.00 pm		†10.48 pm	†10.10 pm		†10.43 pm	†10.15 pm		†10.37 pm		†11.30 pm
†11.00 pm		†11.48 pm	†11.10 pm		†11.43 pm	†11.15 pm		†11.37 pm		

* Daily except Sunday
† Saturday only.

When You Go
Go N. E. O.

We Serve You
Rain or Shine

When You Ship
Ship N. E. O.

We Appreciate
Your
Patronage

NEWS-RECORD PRINT, MIAMI, OKLA.

1933 timetable showed a basic hourly passenger service, the pattern all during the Depression. Runs north into Kansas had been discontinued.
Stephen D. Maguire Collection

Passenger service on the NEO was up-to-date with a small fleet of Cincinnati lightweight cars. Here is car 34 entering the street in North Miami on May 6, 1934.
Robert V. Mehlenbeck

Classic heavyweight interurbans with paired, arched windows came to NEO from the Nashville-Gallatin Interurban. Photo at top shows car 100 with orange body and black roof in the yards at Miami on May 6, 1934. Note bow trolleys, their use made possible by the line's catenary overhead. Bows were extremely rare in the U.S. though common in Europe. Other photo is of car 102 a year later after conversion to work train service.

Both: Robert V. Mehlenbeck

Connecting service at Picher to Joplin was given by the Southwest Missouri Railway, whose lightweight car 91 is shown rounding a corner in downtown Joplin, Missouri, on May 6, 1934. Photo at bottom is similar car of the SWM at the company shops in September 1935. Note Depression-level fare structure: round-trip fare only a nickel more than one way.

Both: Robert V. Mehlenbeck

OKLAHOMA, KANSAS & MISSOURI INTERURBAN RY. CO. (inc. and opened 1908), to OKLAHOMA, KANSAS & MISSOURI RY. (5-18-17)

In 1911, owned 2 steam locomotives, 2 cars. The following gas-electric cars were owned:

FLEET NO.	BUILDER	ORDER	REMARKS
106	Gen.Elec/Wason	3743	Acq 12/1915 Chicago Peoria & St Louis 103; sold 1922 Minnesota Western 36
107	Gen.Elec/Wason	3747	Acq 3/1916 CP&StL 101; orig. GE stock 14. Sold 1922 Electric Short Line 310.
108	Gen.Elec/Wason	3746	Acq 3/1916 CP&StL 102. Sold 1922 Minnesota Western 38.

In 1919 also owned the following nonpowered (trailer) equipment:

201,203,205		Coaches; 205 rebuilt 1920 to baggage car.
305		Combo. These cars lasted to about 1928.

NORTHEAST OKLAHOMA RAILROAD (Electric cars)

FLEET NO.	BUILDER	ORDER	DATE	REMARKS
20,22,24,26	?			DT interurban pass. cars, acq 2nd hand. 20 out early, others out 1926.
100,102	American	937	8-21-12	DT interurban combine. Acq 1921 Union Tcn Co (Nashville-Gallatin) TN.
101,103	American	937	8-21-12	DT interurban combine. Acq 1923 Arkansas Valley Interurban 101 (14),15. Orig. Union Tcn (TN) 201-204 series (see above). Cars were named on NEO: 100 "Piankasha" 101 "Cherokee" 102, 103 unk. 102 kept as line car.
50	?			Express motor. Ex Union Tcn (TN)?
201	Jewett		1908	DT interurban combine. Acq 1922 Joplin-Pittsburg RR 201. Rblt to loco 402.
300-304	Jewett		1907	DT interurban. Acq 1923 Cincinnati & Columbus Tcn Co.
34,36	Cincinnati	2735	1924	DT Lwt interurban. Acq 1933 Northampton Transit 34,36. Out 1940.
1	Bald-West.	52669	12-1919	50t 400hp electric locomotive. New.
2	Bald-West.	54748	5-1921	50t 400hp electric locomotive. New.

NOTE: Both locomotives sold 1941 to CRANDIC (IA) 56-57; sold 1954 Kansas City Kaw Valley 506,505; sold 1962 Iowa Terminal RR (IA) 51-52.

402	NEO Shops		1929	Rblt from combine 201. Scrapped 1940. Electric loco.
257	Gen.Elec.	7297	12-1918	60t elec. locomotive; acq ? from Commonwealth Edison, Chicago IL; sold 1940 Montreal & Sou Counties 327; sold 1952 Oshawa Ry 327. Scrapped 1961.

NORTHEAST OKLAHOMA STEAM LOCOMOTIVES

FLEET NO.	TYPE	CYL.	BUILDER	ORDER	DATE	REMARKS
11	2-8-0		Alco?			2nd Hand. Scrapped 1933.
600?	2-8-0	21x28	Baldwin	18480	12-1900	Acq 12/18/25 via BR&L; ex-Barry Equip Co; Orig. CGW 309.
?	4-6-0		Alco-Schn	43751	9-1907	2nd Hand; ex-LJSmith Const Co 100; Orig. SAL 672. Sold Houston & Brazos Valley 110.

NORTHEAST OKLAHOMA DIESEL LOCOMOTIVES

FLEET NO.	TYPE	HP	WGT	BUILDER	ORDER	DATE	REMARKS
253	B-B D/E	400	80t	Gen.Elec	12187	6-37	Acq 4/1939 Cumm. Eng. Co. Sold to Louisiana Sou Ry 504-505.
254	B-B D/E	400	80t	Gen.Elec	12185	6-37	See above.
255	B-B D/E	400	80t	Gen.Elec	12188	6-37	Acq 4/1939 Cumm. Eng. Co. Sold Republic Steel 196, Massilon OH.
255(2d)	B-B D/E	500	80t	Gen.Elec	12588	5-40	New. Sold to Solvay Process Co (OH) then Allied Chemical & Dye.
256	B-B D/E	500	80t	Gen.Elec	12995	3-41	New. Sold LaSalle & Bureau Co (IL) 7 then Ferguson & Edmonson Co. (Freedom PA) then Eastern Gas & Fuel Assoc 1 (Everett MA).
257	B-B D/E	500	80t	Gen.Elec	17897	4-43	New. Sold 1962 via Pan Amer Eng Co (D) to Johala y Lamina (Mex).
601	B-B D/E	1000	90t	Cumm-GE	100	9-37	Acq 2-9-42 Ft Worth & Denver 601; ex-Wichita Valley 101; Orig. Cumm. demo. Sold for scrap 9-26-46 Iron & Steel Products Co.
703	B-B D/E	1000		Alco-GE	74668	5-46	Model S-2. New. To StLSF 295.
704	B-B D/E	1000		Alco-GE	75383	9-47	Model S-2. New. To StLSF 296.
705	B-B D/E	1000		Alco-GE	77041	2-50	Model S-4. New. To StLSF 297.
706	B-B D/E	1000		Alco-GE	80066	8-52	Model S-4. New. To StLSF 298.

Bibliography

THE FOLLOWING guidebooks, historical books, bulletins, magazine articles and newspaper stories were used as source material for this work:

All-Time Index of Magazines (1929-1969), Wayner Publications, New York, N.Y. (1971).

American Street Railway Investments, McGraw Publishing Co. (1909).

Chronicles of Oklahoma, Spring 1973.

The Commercial & Financial Chronicle, Electric Railway Section, William B. Dana Company, New York, N.Y. (April 1922).

Department of Commerce & Labor, Bureau of the Census. Special Reports Street & Electric Railways 1902. Washington: Government Printing Office, 1905.

The Electric Interurban Railways in America. George W. Hilton and John F. Due, Stanford University Press (1960).

Electric Railway Journal. McGraw-Hill (January 1931).

Marguarite McFadden's unpublished manuscript concerning the Webbers Falls, Shawnee & Western Railroad, Webbers Falls, Oklahoma.

McGraw Electric Railway Directories. McGraw-Hill (1916 through 1924).

McGraw Electric Railway Manual. McGraw Publishing Co. (1912 and 1913).

The Official Guide of the Railways (August 1950, December 1955, January 1958, December 1958, June 1966, June 1970, November 1971).

Poor's Manual of the Railroads (1889 through 1912).

Santa Fe, The Railroad That Built An Empire, James Marshall, Random House (1945).

Short Circuit Bulletin, The Texas Division, Electric Railroaders Association, Milam Building, San Antonio, Texas (1971 and 1972).

The Street Railway Blue Book. North American Blue Book Co., Chicago, Illinois (September 1903).

Traction Fans Directory for 1962. The Vane A. Jones Co., Indianapolis, Indiana.

Traction Heritage. Selections from *Electric Railway Journal,* Indianapolis, Indiana (1909 and 1920).

Transit Industry of the United States, Basic Data and Trends, American Transit Association, New York, N.Y. (1942).

Transit Journal, Public Transportation. City, Suburban and Interurban. McGraw-Hill (January 1932, January 1933, January 1934, January 1935, January 1936, January 1937, January 1938, January 1939, January 1940).

Trolley Car Treasury., Frank Rowsome, McGraw Hill (1956). Stephen D. Maguire, Technical Editor.

Trolley Through the Countryside. Allison Chandler. Sage Books, Denver (1963).

Index

Information in rosters is not indexed.
Numbers in italics indicate photographs.
NOTES: Geographical place names in Oklahoma are shown without name of state; those in other states are shown with state name.